Early English Women Writers 1660-1800

Early English Women Writers 1660-1800

Agnes Beaumont, *The Narrative of the Persecutions of Agnes Beaumont*
(ed. by Vera J. Camden)

Cornelia Knight, *Dinarbas*
(ed. by Ann Messenger)

Eliza Haywood, *Three Novellas*
(ed. by Earla A. Wilputte)

Frances Burney, *The Witlings*
(ed. by Clayton J. Delery)

Priscilla Wakefield, *Mental Improvement*
(ed. by Ann B. Shteir)

PRISCILLA WAKEFIELD

MENTAL IMPROVEMENT

Edited with Introduction and Notes
by Ann B. Shteir

COLLEAGUES PRESS
EAST LANSING

Early English Women Writers 1660-1800: No. 4

ISBN 0-937191-51-5
Library of Congress Catalog Number 94-69451
British Library Cataloguing-in-Publication data available
Copyright 1995 by Ann B. Shteir

Published by Colleagues Press Inc.
Post Office Box 4007
East Lansing, Michigan 48826

Distributed outside North America by
Boydell and Brewer Ltd.
Post Office Box 9
Woodbridge, Suffolk IP12 3DF
England

Printed in the United States of America

CONTENTS

ACKNOWLEDGEMENTS

Work on this volume was funded in part by the Social Sciences and Humanities Research Council of Canada. Mrs. Priscilla Mitchell, a lineal descendant of Priscilla Wakefield, cordially welcomed me, and made family documents available for scholarly study. For guidance and access to materials, I thank Mr. Lawrence Darton, and Malcolm Thomas and other staff members at Friends House Library, London. My thinking about Priscilla Wakefield's *Mental Improvement* benefitted from the curiosity, incredulity, and indignation of students in a Humanities Research Seminar on "Women and Culture" and a Graduate English/Women's Studies course on "Women and Eighteenth-Century Writing." I gratefully acknowledge research assistance from Philippa Schmiegelow, and technical assistance from Hazel O'Loughlin-Vidal and Rita Marinucci, all of York University.

"Except a walk, devoted the day to writing — find amusement as well as profit in the employment and hope to be a humble instrument in conveying instruction to others." (Priscilla Wakefield, *Journal*, April 26, 1799)

Mental Improvement: Or, the Beauties and Wonders of Nature and Art (1794-7) is a generic hybrid of children's literature, conduct literature, didactic literature, and popular science writing. Constructed as a domestic fiction "in a Series of Instructive Conversations," it features a family meeting to talk about topics such as whales, beavers, glass-making, silkworms, ship-building, microscopes, porcelain painting, coral, oak-galls, cloth manufacture, the slave trade, good habits, and time management. The book is an attitudinal treasure-trove, and a compendium of issues that were on the cultural table for writers, parents, and children in England during the late eighteenth century.

The conversationalists in *Mental Improvement* are Mr. and Mrs. Harcourt, their four children aged 9-16, and another girl, a motherless family friend. During the day, the children are with their teachers; the girls have a governess and a writing master. Evenings, if they have done their lessons and have obeyed their mother, they are welcomed into Papa's study. The benevolent father, the formal intellectual authority of the book, sets the topics, delivers "lectures," and calls upon the children to perform. The benevolent mother supplies information on many topics, and also gives moral and spiritual commentary; Mrs. Harcourt "takes pleasure in doing good, and is never better pleased than when she has an opportunity of improving young people" (7).

Mental Improvement was a textbook in its day, not a school-text, but rather one for the broader type of informal education mandated by reformist writers, parents, and publishers. Family historians will discern representations of a "properly" functioning family here. Priscilla Wakefield's nuclear family meets at home, in a spatially self-enclosed world. Their orientation to an ethos of improvement shows the family as a socializing institution within late eighteenth-century industrial and mercantilist society. In many ways the book illustrates Isaac Kramnick's contention that English children's literature at that time inculcated regularity, self-reliance, and industry, in a social gospel of method and hierarchy. The mother in *Mental Improvement* declares, for example, that "[o]rder is, indeed, the best guide in every kind of business, and distinguishes a well taught mind, from one that is unin-structed. It should extend to all our concerns; the disposal of our time and money, the proportion of amusement and business" (31).

The Harcourts illustrate how tightly features of the emergent middle-class family are interwoven with ideas about women, gen-der, class, and religion (Davidoff/Hall). Their sexual politics cele-brate individualism yet contain everything with Father's embrace. Wakefield's domestic fiction in *Mental Improvement* does not chal-lenge the authority of father. The book promises mental and moral enlargement for its readers, particularly for female readers, but enlargement is gendered. Mrs. Harcourt declares, for example, that a young woman "is not expected to be deeply skilled in philoso-phy; much less to display her knowledge, should she possess a small share; but a general acquaintance with the uses of the most common philosophical instruments is not only ornamental, but also a very useful accomplishment, and should form part of every liberal education" (163).

Nevertheless, *Mental Improvement* can also be read as a piece of enabling cultural legislation for female agency. Mrs. Harcourt is more than only a tool in cultural domestication. Instead, she is another of Mitzi Myers's moral mothers in the "mentorial tradi-tion," an exemplar of female agency, who exercises intellectual and moral authority (Myers). Moral Mothers like Mrs. Harcourt abound in women's writing during the 1790s, sometimes subver-sive, usually pragmatic and ameliorist, and not silenced. Tough and demanding, they insist on rationality, especially for women. Thus, when Augusta, the young visitor in *Mental Improvement*, expresses a fear of spiders, Mrs. Harcourt explains that she has been "brought up with this prejudice": "Use your reason, over-come such groundless fears; with men of sense, they lay our sex under the imputation of affectation or ignorance, and savour strongly of vulgarity and want of education" (103). Mrs. Harcourt is meant to exemplify good mothering in a mid-1790s liberal style, combining firmness with affectionate sweetness toward her chil-dren. As the facilitator of the family's intellectual conversations, she arranges the Information Spectaculars that make up *Mental Improvement*, and delivers the last speech in the book. Figures of domestic and maternal female authority like Mrs. Harcourt shaped the instrumental woman's voice, and enabled women to come into voice as writers during the late eighteenth century (Armstrong, Perry, Todd).

In Wakefield's model family, the fulcrum of knowledge is not a male spin-off from Papa, but rather the daughter who can answer every question right. Sophia, the oldest and best-versed child in the Harcourt constellation, has intellectual authority, and represents the success of the family's educational philosophy. Women in Priscilla Wakefield's books learn science and teach it to others; in *Mental Improvement* Mrs. Harcourt and a younger daughter use a microscope to study the structure of bees. Sophia, a learned girl, is particularly adept at botany; there is no moment in the book when her family tries to circumscribe her intellectual agility.

Mental Improvement embodies and discusses ideas about education. The pedagogical and narrative format of the book is presented as something new, a departure from the "unnatural distance" of conventional teaching. The narrative family in the book considers its own conversations to be a model of parent-child relations different, we read in Conversation 15, from the "austere manners of former times [that] secluded children from the advantage of conversing with their parents or instructors." Mrs. Harcourt addresses the matter of style in teaching in this way:

> [T]he familiar intercourse, that is now maintained with young people by their parents, and those who preside over their education, affords them an agreeable opportunity of enlarging their minds, and attaining a fund of knowledge, by the easy medium of conversation. The liberality, with which young persons are treated in the present times, promises still greater hopes of advantage in the culture of the heart and disposition, than in the improvement of the faculties; by substituting real affection and friendship, in lieu of that distant respect, which is only the shadow of it. (118-119)

In the same conversation, Mr. Harcourt remarks upon the "spirit of improvement" behind the educational writings for children at that time, and adds that "various ingenious methods of facilitating the acquisition of knowledge have been invented" (118). Books in the format of dialogues or conversations were prominent among those "ingenious methods."

Priscilla Wakefield, a professional writer at the beginning of her career when *Mental Improvement* was first published, produced books calibrated to different audience levels, and directed some of her books to children, and others to older "youthful minds." Most of her books are familiar/familial narratives, in the form of letters or conversations among family members. Priscilla Wakefield particularly favored conversations between parents and children, set at home before supper, during walks with mother in the garden, or on family trips. Like other eighteenth-century writers, she could draw upon a rich narrative heritage for the dialogue form that reached back to Platonic and Socratic forms, and recalled traditional uses of dialogues in literature, philosophy, pedagogy, and science during the Renaissance and early modern Europe (Cox, Burke). Within eighteenth-century culture, the conversational style figured socially and narratively in gossip and Bluestocking *conversazione* (Cope). Proper conversation belonged to the culture of sociability, and reformers elevated it to the list of approved activities, contrasting conversation with card-playing, for example. Hester Chapone, Bluestocking and educator, promoted serious conversation as a route to virtue; conversation, she wrote, influences "our habits of thinking and acting, and the whole form and colour of our minds,...that which may chiefly determine our character and condition to all eternity" (Chapone, 40). Conversation manuals introduced novices of various social stations to the skills of oral conversation, and often included models of practice (Warren).

Later eighteenth-century teachers and educational writers promoted the pedagogical value of dialogues and conversations. Thus, Ann Murry discussed teaching styles in her courtesy book *Mentoria: or, The Young Ladies Instructor* (1778): "Dialogue and fable are in general esteemed the best vehicles to convey instruction, as they lure the mind into knowledge, and imperceptibly conduct it to the goal of wisdom. This mode of practice often succeeds, where formal precept fails" (xi). Maria Edgeworth explains in *Practical Education* (1798) that "[f]rom conversation, if properly managed, children may learn with ease, expedition, and delight...; and a skilful preceptor can apply in conversation all the principles that we have laboriously endeavoured to make intelligible in a quarto volume" (775).

Priscilla Wakefield's *Mental Improvement* belongs to this pedagogical moment, and embodies the practices it promotes. In general, Priscilla Wakefield's writings record many conversion experiences, in which young people come to see the benefits of activities such as natural history, through which they can learn about moderation, perseverance, diligence, self-command, and toleration. The figure of transformation in *Mental Improvement* is Augusta, a twelve-year-old motherless girl, whose governess provides only formal instruction and whose father takes no part in her general education. She participates in the conversations of the Harcourt family, and is the outsider whose deficiencies prove the value of their household regimen. Rescued by the improving conversations within the Harcourt family, Augusta admits that, had it not been for Mrs. Harcourt, she "must ever have remained ignorant and self-conceited, confirmed in error, a slave to bad habits and...unsubdued passions" (119). Ultimately transformed by natural history, Augusta declares that she wants to become a botanist, just like Sophia.

Priscilla Wakefield was likely one of the women writers that the essayist Charles Lamb complained to Samuel Taylor Coleridge about in 1802 as "that cursed Barbauld Crew" of women writers of didactic books for children about geography and natural history. Charles Lamb, a Romantic and lover of fairy tales, railed against utilitarian education for children, especially the "facts" mentality of an incremental approach to knowledge (Barnett). Priscilla Wakefield embodied that "facts" mentality in many didactic titles written principally for young readers and their families.

At the end of the eighteenth century, when children were an audience to be reckoned with, to be taught and amused through books written especially for them, and when publishers cultivated this newly-defined audience, Priscilla Wakefield joined the company of authors such as Sarah Trimmer, Maria Edgeworth, and Anna Barbauld (Darton, Myers, Pickering). She wrote books on natural history, as well as separate titles on botany and entomology, and was well-known for her volumes of travelogues and moral tales for young people. Her best-selling book *The Juvenile Travellers: containing the remarks of a family during a tour through the principal states and kingdoms of Europe (1801)*, the first of a series of six travel books, went through nineteen editions over the next fifty years. Priscilla Wakefield was doing something deliberately new in shaping travel books and natural history books for juvenile audiences, as she explained in her Preface to *The Juvenile Travellers*:

> It is desirable that children advanced beyond infancy should be acquainted with the prominent features in the character and manners of the inhabitants of other countries,...But, as books of travels are not written for children, they are generally unfit for their perusal, many of them containing passages of an immoral tendency, or treating upon subjects beyond their comprehension. This consideration was the inducement for...information...interwoven with a narrative to engage the attention of young readers without too much diverting them from the main object in view (v).

Priscilla Wakefield's writing for children is one expression of her philanthropic credo of usefulness. She makes frequent anti-slavery pronouncements throughout her writing. In *Mental Improvement*, for example, Conversation 10 concerns the slave trade, with praise of William Wilberforce and remarks on the complicity of England in sending ships to convey slaves, the lack of compassion among the ship captains, and the lack of opportunities for "negroes to improve themselves." The children agree to forego sugar and other products "procured by the sweat of [slaves'] brows," and thereby align themselves with abolitionist boycotting, an act much debated during the 1790s (78; Ferguson, 178-9).

Priscilla Wakefield's teacherly emphases are liberal, moderate feminist, and Quaker. Priscilla Bell Wakefield (1751-1832) grew up in Stamford Hill, Tottenham, Middlesex, and remained a practising, though not uncritical, member of the Society of Friends throughout her life. She herself was "of the world" rather than one of the "close Quakers" who wore Quaker garb and turned away from public amusements such as dancing and the theatre. In her Journal, she records meeting "a crowd of light browns" and being uneasy: "a livery can be no part of Christianity" (June 13, 1799).*
In the late eighteenth century, Tottenham (now part of the London Borough of Haringay) was a prosperous and semi-rural area, four miles north of London, with frequent stagecoach service into the city. There were many Quaker residents, and many schools and charitable institutions established by Friends such as Priscilla Wakefield. Much of her own Friendly energy went into the amelioration of women's lot. She founded a School of Industry for girls, and established a Lying-In Charity for poor women approaching childbirth. She was instrumental in founding a Female Benefit Club to pay small pensions to poor subscribers after age 65; allied to this club were a loan fund, a Penny Bank for encouraging monthly deposits by children of the labouring poor, and a "frugal-

---

* Priscilla Wakefield's Journals date from 1796, 1798, and 1799, with sporadic entries thereafter through 1816. Her Literary Journals date from 1798, and 1804-7, and consist of her comments on books and magazines. These manuscripts, formerly in family hands in England and now in New Zealand, are available in xeroxed form in the Hazel Mews Papers, Library of the Society of Friends, London. A typescript "Life of Priscilla Wakefield" by Lady Chapman draws upon material in the journals as well as upon family sources (xerox in Hazel Mews Papers).

ity bank" for receiving deposits from the adult poor and for paying interest on those funds. These projects belong to the early history of Savings Banks in England. She also supported the Quaker Joseph Lancaster in his attempts to educate large numbers of poor pupils by using a monitorial system of instruction; she and her son Edward lobbied to make Lancaster's ideas known, and to raise money for his schools.*

Priscilla Wakefield had a Friendly impetus to doing good works through her writing, but her step over the threshold into authorship also had a material base. She began writing when she was over forty. Neither a naturalist nor a first-hand traveller to exotic places, she was a deliberate writer, who saw her books as a way to assist the family purse when her husband's business was in difficulty and a younger son was beset by legal expenses. "Necessity," she recorded in her Journal, "obliges me to write." Her books were issued by the radical publisher Joseph Johnson, the juvenile publisher Elizabeth Newbery, and especially by the Quaker publishing firm of Darton and Harvey. In October 1796, when she had completed a dialogue for a work-in-progress, she wondered whether she would be able "to obtain a good price for my labour from Darton"; a few months later she noted having "Finished my bargain with Darton tolerably to my satisfaction." The satisfaction probably was mutual because Darton continued to publish her books, and also gave her books to translate. She continued writing even when financial pressure eased, for she valued work as both potential profit and pleasure. She phrased this in a way common among eighteenth-century intellectual women: "*Employment* a powerful remedy for *uneasiness*" (August 9, 1799).

In 1798 Joseph Johnson published Priscilla Wakefield's book on women's education and women's employment, *Reflections on the Present Condition of the Female Sex, with Suggestions for its Improvement*, her one book exclusively for adults. Priscilla Wakefield, deeply concerned with female dependence throughout her own life, was moved by the plight of others. What, she asks, will become

---

* Credos of usefulness and social service shaped the work of other members of Priscilla Wakefield's family. Edward Wakefield, her older son, wrote about Irish oppression by the British and religious intolerance toward Catholics, supported Arthur Young's work on behalf of agricultural reform, and worked on improving hospital conditions in London. Elizabeth Fry, the prison reformer, was her niece.

of the unsuitably educated woman of the lower middle class when she is widowed and has no training through which to ensure some self-sufficiency for herself? In *Reflections* Wakefield argues that women's education should prepare them for life by teaching them skills linked to their socio-economic class. She offers various schemes for opening up female employment, such as giving women access to farming and the millinery trade. Among the many books on women's education at this time, hers was a book of practical suggestions in a reformist mode, rather than one arguing for large-scale social change.

Priscilla Wakefield began an ameliorative proposal to a periodical by admitting that she was "not a bold Projector" (*Monthly Magazine*, 1800). In decades that highlighted grand gestures, Priscilla Wakefield flew no banners of Sensibility, Jacobinism, or Romanticism. She was an accommodationist, hewing to a path of order, self-control, and decorum. Within the range of views about women in late eighteenth-century England, Priscilla Wakefield lived and worked in the ideological terrain between Mary Wollstonecraft and Hannah More. With neither Mary Wollstonecraft's vision of radical social change nor Hannah More's political conservatism, Wakefield was committed to Reason as the strategy for female improvement, while also accepting class-specific and gender-specific boundaries in activity and behaviour for women.*

---

* Reviewing William Godwin's *Life of Mary Wollstonecraft* in her Literary Journal, Priscilla Wakefield wrote about Mary Wollstonecraft: "Her mind was capacious, her judgment clear...The originality of her genius was not curbed by any regular cultivation, her faculties were left to expand by their own force which probably contributed to leave her free from the actual fetters of prejudice — but whilst this neglect procured her so great an advantage[,] it deprived her of the benefit of early impressions of religious principles. Void of fixed sentiments on this essential subject she deviated from those wholesome and necessary restraints wh[ich] the doctrines of revelation impose upon natural inclination, when it leads beyond those limits wh[ich] the good order of society and happiness require — Possessing those great talents in combination with many enviable qualities of heart she might have formed a model for her sex by her example but unguarded by a sense of religious duty she wandered from that standard of female excellence wh[ich] the Author of the Rights of Women should have defended by a purity of conduct consistent with the perfection she had delineated. Such a combination of great qualities and defects is a humbling lesson and teaches us to qualify our notions of human excellence" (April 4, 1798).

In *Writing Women's Literary History*, Margaret Ezell calls for a feminist historicism that recognizes that "the literary past is much more chaotic and diverse than we have previously implied in our literary histories" (164). Science writing is part of the history of women's writing, and Priscilla Wakefield was among women of her day who featured science in early textbooks, courtesy books, didactic poetry, and children's literature. Her attention to natural history in *Mental Improvement* renders the book a marker in the history of women's popular science writing. For Priscilla Wakefield, science was part of sociability, a way of teaching Enlightenment values, and a versatile resource for women. She belongs to the first generation of women who wrote introductory books on science and natural history for children, women, and a lay public. (Another well-known writer was Jane Marcet.) Her pioneering *Introduction to Botany* (1796) taught about the Linnaean system of plant classification through a series of letters between sisters. It went through many editions in England and America, was translated into French, and was updated in later years to take account of changing ideas about plant taxonomy (Shteir).

Priscilla Wakefield's didactic books enlarge the canon of eighteenth-century writing by blending the informational and familial, and textualizing social history and the history of science culture in fruitful ways. The juxtaposition of *Mental Improvement* with Bernard de Fontenelle's *Conversations on the Plurality of Worlds (1686)* helps to make this point. Fontenelle, a man of letters and a favorite in Parisian salons, later perpetual secretary of the Académie des Sciences, fashioned conversations between a well-versed philosopher and an aristocratic woman about the telescope, the microscope, Cartesian vortices, and Newtonian science. The sparkling and flirtatious dialogues are openly speculative, and are emancipatory in their rhetoric about releasing people from the fetters of superstition. Like *Mental Improvement*, Fontenelle's work uses a conversational format to popularize knowledge. Historical changes in authorship, audience, and political, literary, and cultural climates account for differences between a book by a late seventeenth-century *philosophe* for French aristocratic polite culture and a book by a late eighteenth-century professional woman writer for British children in the middle ranks. Wakefield's family conversations suggest new uses for the dialogue in the late eighteenth century as a progressive form of narrative, one that embodies a new pedagogy and a new family style, and moves science from the salon into the domestic routines of an emergent middle-class where Mother is an educator who shapes access to knowledge.

Priscilla Wakefield had a finger on the pulse of what some audiences across the middle ranks in England and America wanted from didactic children's literature at the turn of the nineteenth century. *Mental Improvement: Or, the Beauties and Wonders of Nature and Art* was a popular and widely reprinted book for three decades. To the original two-volume edition of 1794, Priscilla Wakefield added a third volume when the third edition appeared in 1797. Thereafter, *Mental Improvement* was reprinted ten more times; the thirteenth and last British edition appeared in 1828. The first American edition was issued in 1797; the book reached its fourth American edition in 1819. The *Critical Review, British Critic,* and *Monthly Review* all praised it as an improving book for "the rising generation." A correspondent in the *Monthly Magazine* included it in "a 'Kitchen Library,' for the use of...servants when their work is over" (1798). The *Critical Review* recommended *Mental Improvement* for adults, "who, by a perusal of it, would discover in themselves a degree of ignorance they little suspected" (1795). This Colleagues Press edition of *Mental Improvement* is based upon the original two-volume version from 1794.

WORKS CITED

Armstrong, Nancy. *Desire and Domestic Fiction: A Political History of the Novel*. New York: Oxford University Press, 1986.

Barnett, George L. "'That Cursed Barbauld Crew' or Charles Lamb and Children's Literature," *The Charles Lamb Bulletin*, n.s. 25 (January 1979): 1-18.

Burke, Peter. *The Art of Conversation*. Ithaca: Cornell University Press, 1993.

Chapman, Lady. "A Life of Priscilla Wakefield." Hazel Mews Papers, Library of the Society of Friends, London.

Chapone, Hester. "On Conversation," *Miscellanies in Prose and Verse*. London: E. and C. Dilly, 1775.

Cope, Kevin L. ed. *Compendious Conversations: The Method of Dialogue in the Early Enlightenment*. Frankfurt am Main: Peter Lang, 1992.

Cox, Virginia. *The Renaissance Dialogue: Literary Dialogue in its Social and Political Contexts, Castiglione to Galileo*. Cambridge: Cambridge University Press, 1992.

The Critical Review 15 (1795): 357.

Darton, F.J.Harvey. *Children's Books in England: Five Centuries of Social Life*. Cambridge: Cambridge University Press, 1982.

Davidoff, Leonore & Catherine Hall. *Family Fortunes: Men and Women of the English Middle Class 1780-1850*. Chicago: University of Chicago Press, 1987.

Edgeworth, Maria and Richard Lovell. *Practical Education*. London: J. Johnson, 1798.

Ezell, Margaret J.M. *Writing Women's Literary History*. Baltimore: Johns Hopkins University Press, 1993.

Ferguson, Moira. *Subject to Others: British Women Writers and Colonial Slavery, 1670-1834*. New York: Routledge, 1992.

Fontenelle, Bernard de. *Conversations on the Plurality of Worlds*, trans. H.A. Hargreaves. Berkeley: University of California Press, 1990.

Kramnick, Isaac, "Children's Literature and Bourgeois Ideology: Observations on Culture and Industrial Capitalism in the later 18th Century," *Studies in Eighteenth-Century Culture* 12 (1983): 11-44.

The Monthly Magazine 6 (1798): 355; 10 (1800): 300.

Murry, Ann. *Mentoria: or, The Young Ladies Instructor*. London: C. Dilly, 1778.

Myers, Mitzi. "Impeccable Governesses, Rational Dames, and Moral Mothers: Mary Wollstonecraft and the Female Tradition in Georgian Children's Books," *Children's Literature* 14 (1986): 31-59.

Perry, Ruth. "Colonizing the Breast: Sexuality and Maternity in Eighteenth-Century England," *Journal of the History of Sexuality* 2 (1991): 204-34.

Pickering, Samuel F., Jr. *Moral Instruction and Fiction for Children, 1749-1820.* Athens: University of Georgia Press, 1993.

Shteir, Ann B. *Flora's English Daughters: Women and the Culture of Botany, 1760-1860.* Baltimore: Johns Hopkins University Press (forthcoming).

Todd, Janet. *The Sign of Angelica: Women, Writing and Fiction, 1660-1800.* London: Virago, 1989.

Wakefield, Priscilla. *A Brief Memoir of the Life of William Penn.* London: Darton, Harvey and Darton, 1816.

_____ *Domestic Recreation; or Dialogues Illustrative of Natural and Scientific Subjects.* London: Darton and Harvey, 1805.

_____ *Excursions in North America.* London: Darton and Harvey, 1806.

_____ *A Family Tour through the British Empire.* London: Darton and Harvey, 1804.

_____ *Instinct Displayed in a Collection of Well-Authenticated Facts.* London: Darton, Harvey and Darton, 1811.

_____ *Introduction to Botany.* London: E. Newbery, 1796.

_____ *Introduction to the Natural History and Classification of Insects.* London: Darton, Harvey and Darton, 1816.

_____ Journals 1796-1816, and Literary Journals, 1798, 1804-7. Hazel Mews Papers, Library of the Society of Friends, London.

_____ *Juvenile Anecdotes, Founded on Facts.* London: Darton and Harvey, 1795-8.

_____ *The Juvenile Travellers; containing the Remarks of a Family during a Tour through the Principal States and Kingdoms of Europe.* London: Darton and Harvey, 1801.

_____ *Leisure Hours, or Entertaining Dialogues between Persons Eminent for Virtue and Magnanimity.* London: Darton and Harvey, 1794-6.

_____ *Perambulations in London, and its Environs.* London: Darton & Harvey, 1809.

_____ *Reflections on the Present Condition of the Female Sex.* London: J. Johnson, 1798; rpt. New York: Garland, 1974.

_____ *Sketches of Human Manners, delineated in Stories.* London: Darton, Harvey & Co., 1807.

_____ *The Traveller in Africa*. London: Darton, Harvey and Darton, 1814

_____ *The Traveller in Asia*. London: Darton, Harvey and Darton, 1817.

_____ *Variety; or Selections and Essays consisting of Anecdotes, Curious Facts, and Interesting Narratives*. London: Darton, Harvey & Co., 1809.

Warren, Leland. "Turning Reality Round Together: Guides to Conversation in Eighteenth-Century England," *Eighteenth Century Life* n.s. 8 (1983): 65-87.

Mental Improvement:

OR THE

BEAUTIES AND WONDERS

OF

NATURE AND ART,

CONVEYED

IN A SERIES OF

INSTRUCTIVE CONVERSATIONS.

BY

PRISCILLA WAKEFIELD,

AUTHOR OF LEISURE HOURS.

VOL. I.

LONDON:

PRINTED AND SOLD BY DARTON AND HARVEY,
NO. 55, GRACECHURCH-STREET.

M.DCC.XCIV.

PREFACE

The art of exercising the faculty of thinking and reflection upon every object that is seen, ought to constitute a material branch of a good education; but it requires the skill of a master's hand, to lead the minds of youth to the habit of observation. Dr. Watts* says, that there are four methods of attaining knowledge: Observation, reading, conversation, and meditation. The first lies within the compass even of children, and from the early dawn of reason, they should be accustomed to observe every thing with attention, that falls under their notice. A judicious instructor will find matter for a lesson among those objects, that are termed common or insignificant. How little this is generally the case, may be collected from the ignorance, not of children only, but sometimes of youth, who, although they have attained a considerable degree of classical learning, are unacquainted either with the materials of those things they daily use, or the methods of manufacturing them. The form and appearance of substances are so much changed by the effects of art, that it would be impossible for a mind, unprepared by instruction, to conceive the original material of many things, that are in the most common use. Would any child suppose, that the cloth, of which her frock is made, is composed of the fibrous parts of a green plant; or that the paper upon which she draws is the same substance wrought into a different form; that the transparent glass out of which she drinks, was once a heap of sand and ashes; or that the ribbon she wears is the produce of an insect? The design of the following little work, is to excite the curiosity of young persons on these subjects, by furnishing information on a few of the most obvious. The form of dialogue has been adopted as best suited to convey instruction blended with amusement; being desirous that it should be read rather from choice than compulsion, and be sought by my young readers as an entertainment, not shunned as a mere dry preceptive lesson.

---

* Rev. Isaac Watts, hymn-writer and author of *Divine Songs...in easy language for the use of children* (1715), also wrote educational manuals, including *The Improvement of the Mind: or, a Supplement to the Art of Logic* (1741).

THE PERSONS

Mr. HARCOURT.
Mrs. HARCOURT.
SOPHIA, aged sixteen.
CECILIA, aged twelve.
AUGUSTA, an occasional visitor, aged twelve.
CHARLES, aged fifteen.
HENRY, aged nine.

MENTAL IMPROVEMENT:

IN A SERIES OF

INSTRUCTIVE CONVERSATIONS.

CONVERSATION 1

Sophia and Cecilia.

SOPHIA.

HOW happy are we, my dear sister, to be blessed with such parents, who devote so much time to our instruction and amusement! with what tenderness do they listen to our conversation, and improve every subject that arises to our advantage!

CECILIA.

I am never so happy in any other company; they have the art of rendering instruction and study agreeable. Though I tenderly love my governess, I feel such a superior attachment to my mamma, that I am not able to express it; and I am sure Mrs. Selwyn will not blame me for it, for she always advises me to look up to my father and mother as my best and kindest friends.

5

SOPHIA.

Mrs. Selwyn, our worthy governess, is too wise and discreet to be jealous of our preferring our parents to every body; she would sooner direct us to regulate our affections properly, and undoubtedly give them the first place.

CECILIA.

What bitter repentance do I feel, when I have done any thing to offend them, particularly when I am inattentive to their instruction! How comes it, Sophia, that I am so often idle, and my thoughts wander from what I am about, when I really intend to be good?

SOPHIA.

You are very young, my dear, and mamma says that the habit of attention is difficult to form; but that by steadily endeavouring to fix our thoughts on one object we shall every day find it more easy; and though it may cost us some pains at first, let us remember what we owe to the affectionate care of such a mother, and give our whole attention, when she condescends to instruct us.

CECILIA.

I often pity poor Augusta; she has no mamma, and her governess seldom teaches her any thing but her regular lessons.

SOPHIA.

I both love and pity her; she is of a good disposition, but has not received the same advantages that we have; her papa is engaged in business, and leaves her wholly to the care of her governess, who takes but little pains with her.

CECILIA.

Let us desire our parents to give us leave to invite her often to be present at our evening conversations. Papa has promised to give us some account of various manufactures; all will be new to her, she will be delighted, and it will be a means of supplying her with some of the instruction she wants.

SOPHIA.

Mamma will be very willing, I dare say: she takes pleasure in doing good, and is never better pleased than when she has an opportunity of improving young people.

CECILIA.

I long for the evening, when we are all to meet in the study. I wonder what will be the subject papa will have prepared for us. My brothers too are to be of the party, and when we have been separated all day, it is such a pleasure to meet them, that I cannot say how delighted I am with the thoughts of it.

SOPHIA.

It is almost time to attend our writing master, and do not let us forget the terms of admission to these agreeable evening conversations; attention to our lessons in the day, and obedience to the commands of our dear mamma, are the only methods of obtaining a seat in the study at night. Papa will not confine the subject of his lectures wholly to manufactures, but intends to explain the nature of the materials of what we wear and use, which will frequently lead him to describe objects of natural history, a study of which I am particularly fond.

CECILIA.

We are also sometimes to supply a subject, we are to have books given us, that we may be prepared, and are to be questioned on the given subject. I wish I may be able to answer properly.

SOPHIA.

Hark! the bell rings for writing; we must attend the summons.

CONVERSATION 2

Mr. Harcourt, Mrs. Harcourt, Augusta, Sophia,
Cecilia, Charles, and Henry.

Mrs. HARCOURT.

MY dear Augusta, I am glad to see you; my girls tell me you desire to be of our party, when we meet of an evening. Your company will be always agreeable to me, and I hope our conversations will be instructive to you.

AUGUSTA.

I accept the invitation with pleasure; but I hope to receive entertainment as well as instruction; for I shall never be able to attend to a long dry lecture, without some amusement to render it palatable.

Mr. HARCOURT.

I have chosen the Whale for our subject to night, and the information it affords I expect will be new and wonderful to you all.

CHARLES.

Is not the Whale found in the seas towards the north pole?

Mr. HARCOURT.

Yes, my dear, they chiefly inhabit the seas towards the north pole; though many whales are caught in the South Seas towards that pole; but the chief fishery has been near the coast of Spitzbergen, Nova Zembla, and Greenland; where many ships from this country go every year, for the sole purpose of catching whales.

Mrs. HARCOURT.

We may admire the goodness of Providence, who leaves not the most obscure corner of the globe without its peculiar riches. These countries, which scarcely supply food for their wretched inhabitants, and are covered with snow, full nine months in the year, are visited by people from different parts of the world, who brave every danger, for the sake of taking the whales, which are found in their seas.

8

CECILIA.

I cannot think what use they can be of, to tempt people to go so far for them.

Mr. HARCOURT.

You will find that they supply several useful articles for our convenience. Your stays, for example, would not be so well shaped without whalebone.

CECILIA.

Are the bones that stiffen our stays really the bones of whales?

Mr. HARCOURT.

The substance called whalebone, adheres to the upper jaw, and is formed of thin parallel laminae, called whiskers; some of the longest are four yards in length; they are surrounded by long strong hair, to guard the tongue from being hurt, and also to prevent the return of their food, when they discharge the water out of their mouth.

HENRY.

Whiskers four yards long! how fierce the whale must look! pray what size is he himself?

Mr. HARCOURT.

The common whale is the largest of all animals, of whose history we have any certain account; it is sometimes found ninety feet long, and those which inhabit the torrid zone are said to be much larger. The size of the head is about one-third of the whole fish, the under lip is much broader than the upper, which is narrow and oblong, the tongue is a soft, spongy, fat substance, sometimes yielding five or six barrels of oil; the gullet or swallow is very small for so large an animal, not exceeding four inches in width; but that is proportioned to the food it eats, which is a particular kind of small snail; or, as some say, it varies its repast with the Medusa, or sea blubber, an insect which is found in the sea.

SOPHIA.

Is not the whale a fish of prey then? I thought it would devour men, if they unhappily fell in their way.

Mr. HARCOURT.

They are quite harmless and inoffensive to every thing but insects. The only danger to be apprehended from them, is the starting of a plank in a ship, or the overturning of a boat, with their huge bulk.

AUGUSTA.

Oh terrible! what can induce men to incur such dangers, when they may stay quietly at home and enjoy themselves?

Mrs. HARCOURT.

There are many strong reasons that prevail with thousands to undergo a life of hardship, toil, and danger. The necessity of earning a living, to which you, who are brought up in the enjoyment of plenty, are strangers, is one strong inducement.

SOPHIA.

But I would choose some easier employment; a gardener has an agreeable life.

Mr. HARCOURT.

But do you not reflect that all men cannot be gardeners; there is employment for but few in that line. Providence has wisely endued mankind with as great a variety of inclinations and pursuits, as there is diversity in their persons; some show a very early inclination for a sea-life, that no danger can deter, or persuasions prevail with them to give up; which appears to be implanted for the purpose of providing the means of an intercourse between the inhabitants of distant countries, by which each party may reap advantage by interchanging the superfluous produce of distant climes, and exercising the mutual good offices of love and kindness. But to return to the whale; it has two orifices in the middle of the head, through which it spouts water to a great height, and, when it is disturbed or wounded, with a noise like thunder. Its eyes are not larger than those of an ox, and placed at a great distance from each other. There is no fin on the back, but on the sides, under each eye are two large ones which serve it for rowing. The colour varies, the back of some being red, others black, and another variety is mottled; the belly is generally white. They are extremely beautiful in the water; the skin is very smooth and slippery. Under the skin the whale is covered with fat or blubber, from six to twelve

10

inches thick, which sometimes yields from one to two hundred barrels of oil. All Europe is supplied with oil for lamps, and many other purposes, from this blubber. The flesh is red and coarse, somewhat like beef; the Greenlanders eat it, and the Icelanders soak it in sour whey.

CHARLES.

It must be very disagreeable food. I should think, the oil would make it very greasy and strong.

Mr. HARCOURT.

So it does; but the poor people, who live in countries so far north, have but little variety of meat to tempt their appetite. In winter, as your mother has already remarked, the ground is covered with snow, and affords no vegetation but a little moss, which is found on the bodies of trees, consequently the larger animals, such as cattle, &c. cannot subsist there. The reindeer is peculiar to those parts, and supplies his master with a scanty provision during that dreary season; but as they are valuable for many other purposes, they are unwilling to kill them, but from necessity; the flesh of the whale is therefore reckoned a dainty, which may afford us a lesson, to be contented with beef and mutton, and to discourage that spirit of gluttony and sensual indulgence, that prevails too glaringly at the tables of the rich, who are seldom satisfied with one or two plain dishes, but cover their tables with a profusion that invites a false appetite, and wastes the good things that are provided for our use.

CHARLES.

Do whales ever stray so far from their usual haunts, as to be found on our coasts? it would give me great pleasure to see one.

Mr. HARCOURT.

There have been instances of a few, that have been left at low water on shore, but they occur but seldom; when it happens, they are called royal fish, and become the property of the king and queen. Notwithstanding its vast size, the whale swims swiftly, and generally against the wind. The female brings but one, or at most two young ones at a time, which are nine or ten feet long; they suckle their young, and if pursued, shew the same maternal solicitude for the preservation of their offspring, as land animals, by wrapping them up in their fins close to their bodies.

SOPHIA.

Pray, does the whale yield any other produce, that is useful to man, except oil and whalebone?

Mr. HARCOURT.

Yes; Spermaceti is prepared from the oil that is found in the head of a whale. It is melted over a gentle fire, and put into moulds, like those wherein sugar loaves are formed; when cold and drained, it is taken out, and melted over again, till it be well purified and whitened; it is then cut with a knife into flakes, and is used as a medicine for various complaints of the lungs; it is also used for making candles, which are but little inferior to those made of wax.

CHARLES.

I cannot imagine what means can be devised to catch and manage an animal of such prodigious size.

Mr. HARCOURT.

No animal is so large or powerful, but must yield to the superior sagacity of man. The method of taking whales is truly curious, and I shall have pleasure in entertaining you with a recital of it.

ALL.

Pray begin, we are all attention.

Mr. HARCOURT.

The fleet usually sets sail about the beginning of April, and steers northward, till they reach about the 75th degree of north latitude, where they usually begin to meet with the ice. It is among these huge heaps of ice, that float about in these seas, that they find the whale, and there most of the vessels take their station for the fishing. In the English whale fishery, every ship has six or seven boats belonging to it, each of which has one harpooner, one man to steer, one to manage the line, and four seamen to row it; each boat is provided with two or three harpoons, several lances, and six lines fastened together, each one hundred and twenty fathoms long. To each harping iron is fastened a strong stick, about six feet long, and a soft pliable line of as many fathom, called the fore ganger, which is fastened to the lines in the boat. The instrument with which the whale is struck, is a harping iron, or javelin, pointed with steel, in a triangular shape, like the barb of an arrow. The harpooner, upon sight of the fish, flings the harping iron with all his might against its back; and if he be so fortunate as to penetrate the skin and fat into the flesh, he lets go a line fastened to the harping iron, at the end of which is a gourd, which swimming on the water, discovers where the whale is: for, the minute he is wounded, he plunges to the bottom, commonly swimming against the wind; and this is the moment of danger, lest he should outrun the length of the line, and pull the boat after him into the deep; to guard against this inconvenience, a man is fixed by the line with a sharp knife, ready to cut it in a moment, in case of necessity. If the whale returns for air to breathe, the harpooner takes the opportunity to give him a fresh wound, till fainting by loss of blood, from repeated wounds, the men seize that moment for approaching him, and thrusting a long steel lance under his gills, into his breast, and through the intestines, soon dispatch him. When the carcase begins to float, they cut holes in the fins and tail, and tying a rope in them, tow him to the vessel, where he is fastened to the larboard side of the ship, floating upon his back, almost level with the sea.

CHARLES.

What wonderful skill and dexterity are requisite in a Greenland sailor! I should like to make one voyage with them.

Mrs. HARCOURT.

Your curiosity and ardour are excited by the account your father has given us of their expeditions, but you are not aware of the hardships they undergo from the severity of these northern climates.

AUGUSTA.

I have been accustomed to look with contempt on such people, as greatly my inferiors; but, for the future, I will try to respect every body whose employments are useful.

Mr. HARCOURT.

You will do right; for a Greenland whale catcher is a much more valuable member of society, than an idle man of fortune, who lives

13

on the labours of others. In order to take the blubber or fat, from which they procure the oil, and the fins, as they are called, or whalebone, several men get upon the fish, equipped with a kind of iron caulkers or spurs, to prevent their slipping, and cut off the tail, which is hoisted on deck, and then cut square pieces of blubber, weighing two or three thousand pounds, which are hoisted on board with the capstan, where each piece is again divided into smaller pieces, of two or three hundred pounds weight, then these are thrown into the hold, and left for a few days to drain. When all the blubber is cut from off the belly of the fish, it is turned on one side, by means of a piece of blubber, left in the middle, called the cant or turning piece; they cut out the sides in large pieces, which they call hockies. The next operation is to cut out the two large jaw bones, situated in the under lip, which when hoisted on deck, are cleaned, and fastened to the shrouds, with tubs placed under them to catch the oil which they discharge. The carcase is left to float, and supplies food for Greenland birds, called mallemuck, &c. After the pieces of blubber have lain a few days in the hold, they hoist them on deck, cut them into small pieces, and put them through the bung holes into their casks; one of the largest fish will fill more than seventy butts. The produce of a good large whale is valued at about one thousand pounds. When thus richly laden, they begin to sail homewards with their spoil: on their return, the fat is to be boiled, and melted down into train-oil. The whale fishery begins in May, and continues through the months of June and July. Whether the ships are successful or not, they must come away, and get clear of the ice before the end of August.

SOPHIA.

I thank you, my dear papa, for this very entertaining account. I shall never see a piece of whalebone, but I shall think of the labours and difficulties of the poor Greenland sailors.

CHARLES.

I admire the courage and ingenuity of those who first attempted to catch whales.

Mr. HARCOURT.

Probably accident discovered the use that might be made of them, and induced some needy bold adventurer to make the attempt; but many must have been the hazards and disappointments, before the art was reduced to a system, as it is now. Rude and imperfect is the beginning of all knowledge. Perseverance and experience have contributed more than genius, to the discovery of things useful, to accommodate the life of man.

Mrs. HARCOURT.

Much is due to the man who first ventured his life to procure so useful a commodity as train oil, without which, many must pass a long dreary winter's night, without even the cheering rays of a lamp.

HENRY.

But, mamma, they can buy candles.

Mrs. HARCOURT.

Candles, indeed are very useful; but oil is cheaper, and there would not be a sufficient quantity of tallow to light our streets of a night. All the cities in Europe are lighted with oil, which is a great accommodation to their respective inhabitants.

CECILIA.

Are there no other fisheries you can give us an account of, papa?

Mr. HARCOURT.

Yes, my dear, the cod, herring, and salmon fisheries are very useful and extensive, and employ a great number of hands; but our conversation has held long enough for one time, we will reserve them for the subject of another evening.

Mrs. HARCOURT.

It is almost supper time, and little Henry seems ready for bed.

HENRY.

Indeed, mamma, I am not very sleepy, and could sit a great while longer to hear papa tell us more about these huge whales, and mountains of ice.

Mr. HARCOURT.

I will oblige you another time. It is too late now. Adieu, my dear children.

15

CONVERSATION 3

Mr. and Mrs. Harcourt, Augusta, Sophia, Cecilia, Charles, and Henry.

CECILIA.

WE have all waited with the greatest impatience for the hour of meeting. If the cod and herring fisheries afford us as much entertainment as the catching of whales, we shall not soon be tired.

Mrs. HARCOURT.

I am glad to hear you were pleased with last night's conversation; it is a proof that your minds are capable of relishing rational amusement. An early habit of trifling is difficult to be subdued, and should be carefully avoided; thousands are rendered unhappy by it; for having never been accustomed to exercise their faculties, as they grow up, they find everything fatiguing that requires reflection, and as the mind cannot rest wholly inactive, they fly from one trifling, useless pursuit to another; always tired of themselves, and rendering no benefit to others; but a well-regulated mind is marked by the judicious disposal of time, converting even amusement into instruction. Nature and art present so many objectives, calculated to amuse and interest, that none but the idle need want a succession of employment.

AUGUSTA.

Pray, have the kindness to instruct me how to fill up my time. I am often so much at a loss what to do with myself, that I wish for night, to put an end to the long day. As soon as my lessons are over, and nothing can be more tiresome than they are, I am without employment, and wander about without knowing what to do with myself. My governess says, that I must not be troublesome to her, after I have finished my tasks; so I have no body to converse with, nor any thing to amuse me, but playing about, till I am tired.

Mrs. HARCOURT.

Come to us every evening; I hope our conversations will furnish you with many sources of entertainment for your leisure hours. I am willing to point out whatever may occur worthy your further attention, and by strictly adhering to a few simple rules, you will find the day become as short as you wish it.

16

AUGUSTA.

Pray give me these rules. I shall willingly adopt them.

Mrs. HARCOURT.

Perhaps it will not be so easy, at first, as you imagine; ill habits are difficult to surmount; but by degrees it will become familiar, and in time agreeable. In the first place, never be unemployed; read, draw, work, walk, and accustom yourself to observe every thing you see with attention; consider how they are made, what the materials are, and from whence they come. If you are unable to discover the answers, keep a little book, and make a memorandum of what you want to know, and we will endeavour to give you information. This alone will fill many an hour, that now passes tediously away.

AUGUSTA.

I thank you for these directions, and will begin tomorrow; but I have hindered Mr. Harcourt from beginning his account of the cod.

Mr. HARCOURT.

The cod is a fish of passage, and is found from eighteen inches to three or four feet long, with a great head, and teeth in the bottom of the throat, its flesh white, its skin brownish on the back, and covered with a few transparent scales. It eats excellent, when fresh; and if well prepared and salted, will keep a long time. Salt-fish or stock-fish, commonly eaten in Lent, is cod thus prepared. There are two kinds of salt cod, the one called green or white, the other dried or cured. The most essential thing in the green cod-fishery, is the skill of the persons employed to open the fish, to cut off the heads, and to salt them, upon which last the success of the voyage chiefly depends. The principal fishery for cod is on the banks of Newfoundland, in North America; and the best season, from the beginning of February to the end of April, when the cod, which during the winter, had retired to the deepest part of the sea, return to the bank, and grow very fat. Each fisher takes but one cod at a time, yet the more experienced will catch from three hundred and fifty, to four hundred every day. This is a very fatiguing employment, both on account of the weight of the fish, and the extreme cold which reigns on the bank. They salt the cod on board. The head being cut off, the belly opened, and the guts taken out, the salter ranges them in the bottom of the vessel, head to tail, and having thus made a layer of them, a fathom or two square, he covers them with salt, over this he places another layer of fish, which he covers as before; and thus he disposes all the fish of that day, taking care never to mix the fish of different days together. By the time they have lain three or four days thus to drain, they are removed into another part of the vessel, and salted again; then they are left untouched till the ship has got its load, unless they put them in barrels for the conveniency of room.

SOPHIA.

The curing and taking of cod must be less disagreeable and dangerous than whale-catching. I had no idea that the catching of fish alone employed so many men.

Mrs. HARCOURT.

We are apt to use and consume the necessaries and conveniencies of life, without reflecting on the pains and labour necessary to obtain them. The smallest domestic accommodation is frequently not to be had, without the assistance of several hands; a pin or needle, for instance, employs a great number of workmen, before they are brought to the degree of perfection in which we receive them. And the supply of a common table, if we consider the resources from which it is drawn, most probably employs the time and labour of thousands; but we interrupt your father from proceeding, this subject may be resumed another time.

Mr. HARCOURT.

In the fishing for dry cod, vessels of various sizes are used, though such are generally chosen as have large holds, because this kind of fish encumbers more than it burthens. As cod can only be dried by the sun, the European vessels are obliged to put out in March or April, in order to have the benefit of the summer for drying. Indeed the English send vessels for cod later, but they only purchase of the inhabitants what had been caught and prepared before hand. In exchange for which, we carry them meal, brandies, biscuits, pulse, molasses, linen, &c. The fish chosen for this purpose, though the same species as the green cod, is yet much smaller. As soon as the captains arrive, they unrig all the vessels, leaving nothing but the shrouds to sustain the masts; and, in the mean while, the mates provide a tent on shore, covered with branches of fir, and sails over them, with a scaffold, fifty or sixty feet long, and about one-third as broad. While the scaffold is making ready, the crew are fishing, and as fast as they catch, they bring their fish, open them, and salt them on moveable benches; but the main salting is performed on the scaffold, called flake. When the fish have taken salt, they wash them, and lay them on piles on the galleries of the scaffold, to drain again; when sufficiently drained, they are ranged on hurdles, a fish thick, head against tail, with the back uppermost: observing, while they lie thus, to turn and shift them four times every twenty-four hours. When they begin to dry, they lay them in heaps of ten or twelve a piece, to retain their warmth, and continue to enlarge the heap every day, till it becomes double its first bulk. At length they join two of these heaps into one, which they turn every day as before; lastly, salt them over again, beginning with those that had been salted first, and in this state lay them in huge piles, as big as hayricks; and thus they remain till they are carried on ship board, where they are laid on branches of trees, disposed for that purpose, in the bottom of the vessel, with mats around them, to prevent their contracting any moisture. There are four kinds of commodities drawn from cod; the zounds, which is a jelly like substance, that covers the inside of the main bone, and the tongues are salted at the same time with the fish, and barrelled up for eating. The roes or eggs being salted and barrelled, are useful to cast into the sea, to draw fish together, particularly pilchards; and lastly the oil, which is used in dressing of leather; and thus, by the art and ingenuity of man, every part of this fish, that can be serviceable is put to use; and by his skill in curing and drying it, a large supply of wholesome provision is preserved, which must otherwise be lost. Nor is this care bestowed on the cod alone; the herring supplies food to vast numbers of families, especially the poorer sort, to whom they are a great relief, when other provisions are dear; but perhaps you are all tired of this subject, and wish to hear no more concerning the catching of fish; if that be not the case, the herring, though a small fish, will furnish us with wonders almost as extraordinary as the whale.

HENRY.

I am the youngest of the company, and I am not at all tired.

CHARLES.

You surprise me by talking of wonders concerning the herring; I have seen many of them, but never observed any thing in them to excite my attention, beyond fish in common.

Mr. HARCOURT.

It is not any thing remarkable in the construction of the individual fish, to which I allude, but to the prodigious numbers in which they assemble, at certain seasons of the year. About the beginning of June, a shoal of herrings, in bulk not less than the whole extent of Great Britain and Ireland, comes from the north, on the surface of the sea; their approach is known to the inhabitants of Shetland (an island to the north of Scotland) by several tokens in the air and water, as by the birds, such as gannets, &c. which follow, in order to prey upon them; and by the smoothness of the water. It is not certainly known whence they come, though it is probable, that their winter rendezvous is within the arctic circle, where the seas swarm with insect food in greater abundance than in our warmer latitudes. They cast their spawn, when they arrive in these seas, for they come to us full, and are shotten long before they leave us. The great shoal divides into columns of five or six miles in length, and three or four in breadth, reflecting, in bright weather, as they pass, many splendid colours.

SOPHIA.

Well might you say, you had wonderful things to relate; I had formed no idea of shoals of fish of such prodigious extent. The astonishing particulars we have already heard, make me suppose that the sea and its produce, would furnish us with an inexhaustible fund of entertainment.

Mr. HARCOURT.

The subject is too extensive for our limits; the wonders of the deep have not yet been fully explored; but the most obvious particulars, that are ascertained, I shall with pleasure relate, as they illustrate and confirm our notions of the wisdom and goodness of that divine Being, who careth for all the works of his creation, and has provided for the respective wants of each.

CECILIA.

Pray, papa, what kind of fish is the herring? I am not at all acquainted with it.

Mr. HARCOURT.

The herring is a small salt-water fish with a bluish back, and a white silvered belly. It is commonly said that nobody ever saw a

20

herring alive, they die so immediately on being taken out of the water; but there have been instances to the contrary. By what I have already told you, you will perceive that the herring is a fish of passage; they go chiefly in shoals, and are fond of following any fire or light; indeed, as they pass, they resemble a kind of lightning themselves, their colours glancing against the sun. The method of pickling and curing herrings is simple; there are two ways of doing it, the one makes white or pickled herring, the other what is called red herring. The white or pickled herring is prepared by cutting open and gutting the fish, as soon as it is taken out of the water, but the melts and roes are always left in; they are then washed in fresh water, and left for twelve or fifteen hours in a tub full of strong brine, made of fresh water and sea salt. They are then taken out and drained, and when well drained, put up in barrels, disposed evenly in rows or layers, pressed well down, and a layer of salt strewed over them at top and bottom. After washing, gutting, and salting the fish, as above, when they intend to make them red herrings, they string them by the head, on little wooden spits, and hang them in a kind of chimney, made for the purpose, and when the chimney is filled, which generally requires ten or twelve thousand fish, they make a fire underneath of brush-wood, which yields much smoke, but no flame, which mostly dries them sufficiently in twenty-four hours; they are then barrelled for keeping. These are the most important fisheries, and employ by far the greatest number of people; though there are many poor men who live on the sea coasts, whole scanty subsistence depends on the dangerous and precarious employment of fishing; a little boat is their chief treasure, in which they venture out in rough and boisterous weather, when the pressing wants of their family urge them to the undertaking.

Mrs. HARCOURT.

Their danger and hardships are increased, by being obliged to struggle with rough weather, and the storms of winter, that being the principal season for fishing.

CECILIA.

The sufferings of the poor are very great on shore, in cold weather: their miserable huts and tattered cloaths, scarcely defending them from the sharpness of the air, not to mention their scarcity of fuel. I wonder how they support such hardships.

21

Mrs. HARCOURT.

Aged persons and infants sometimes sink under these difficulties, but those in middle life, who are able to use exercise, support
them with less injury. Let these reflections instruct us to feel for the
wants of others, and endeavour to relieve them by retrenching our
superfluous indulgencies; they should inspire us at the same time
with gratitude to the Giver of all Good, for the numerous blessings
he has allotted us, above many other of our fellow creatures: with
thankful acknowledgement, let us close the day, and each one
retire to repose.

CONVERSATION 4

CHARLES.

I HAVE found the subject of the fisheries so new and entertaining, that far from being tired of them, my curiosity is raised to hear more of them. When you returned from Ireland, I think you mentioned having visited the salmon fisheries; be so kind as to give us the particulars you remember of them.

Mr. HARCOURT.

The salmon is a very curious fish, its instinct and habits are well worth our attention. The principal salmon leaps (as they are called) in Ireland, are at Coleraine, and at Ballyshannon, which is a small town situated near the sea, with a bridge of fourteen arches over a river, which at a small distance, falls down a ridge of rocks about twelve feet, and at low water forms a very picturesque cascade.

HENRY.

Do the salmon abound in that river? It must be very pretty to see them tumble down the waterfall.

Mr. HARCOURT.

Almost all the rivers, lakes, and brooks in this island afford great plenty of these fish; some during the whole year, and some only during certain seasons; they generally go down to the sea about August and September, and come up again in the spring months; and, what is very remarkable, the same fish always come back to the same river, so that the owners of the fishery are not afraid of losing their fish.

SOPHIA.

Fish appear so stupid, and void of intelligence, that extraordinary instincts in them strike one with more wonder than in other animals.

Mr. HARCOURT.

The great Creator has impressed certain propensities so strongly on different animals, that they are irresistible; and this powerful inclination stands them in stead of reason, which is given to man, as a being of a superior order, to guide his judgment and direct his conduct through the various scenes of life.

CHARLES.

What inducement can these fish have for thus changing the place of their habitation?

Mr. HARCOURT.

Fresh water seems to be more suitable, than the sea, for depositing their eggs and rearing their young. It is said that the females work beds in the sandy shallows of rivers, and there lay their eggs, which the male impregnates; afterwards they both are employed in covering the eggs with sand, each partaking in the labour necessary for bringing the eggs to perfection; these in time become vivified, and take their course to the sea, being then about four inches long. After a stay of six weeks, or two months, they return up the same rivers; the salt water having caused them to attain nearly to half their full growth, in that short space of time.

Mrs. HARCOURT.

Salmon, and perhaps many other kinds of fish, seem absolved, by the laws of nature, from the sedulous attention in rearing their young, that is requisite in birds and terrestrial animals; their chief care is to provide for the preservation of the eggs, by depositing them in a suitable place, and after they have performed that office, they appear to have no farther thought about them. Strangers to the pleasing solicitude of parental fondness, they may with propriety be ranked in an inferior scale of existence to the beautiful feathered race, whose tenderness and patient care may serve as models to careless mothers, who neglect their offspring, from indolence, or a love of other pursuits.

Mr. HARCOURT.

When I was at Ballyshannon, I passed several hours in watching the fish leap up the cascade, and it is hardly credible, but to those who have been eye-witnesses, that they should be able to dart themselves near fourteen feet perpendicularly out of the water; and, allowing for the curvature, they leap at least twenty. They do not always succeed at the first leap; sometimes they bound almost to the summit, but the falling water dashes them down again; at other times they dart head-foremost, or side-long upon a rock, remain stunned for a few moments, and then struggle into the water again; when they are so successful as to reach the top, they swim out of sight in a moment. They do not bound from the surface of the water, and it cannot be known from what depth they take their leap; it is probably performed by a forcible spring with their tails bent; for the chief strength of most fish lies in the tail. They have often been shot, or caught with strong barbed hooks fixed to a pole, during their flight, as it may be termed; and instances have been known of women catching them in their aprons. At high water, the fall is hardly three feet, and then the fish swim up that easy acclivity without leaping. Sometimes I have seen at low water fifty or sixty of these leaps in an hour, and at other times only two or three. I placed myself on a rock on the brink of the cascade, so that I had the pleasure of seeing the surprising efforts of these beautiful fish close to me; and at the bottom of the fall, porpoises and seals tumbling and playing among the waves; and sometimes a seal carries off a salmon under his fins.

AUGUSTA.

I knew a boy of nine years old, who lived in Scotland, where the rivers are remarkably clear; he saw a salmon sporting in the water at the bottom of his father's garden, and jumped in. The fish was large and strong, and struggled to escape from his hold; but after a pretty smart contest, the boy came off victorious, and brought his antagonist safe to land.

HENRY.

That must have been fine sport; I should like to have been of the party.

CHARLES.

This account is very entertaining; but I want to know their method of taking these fish.

Mr. HARCOURT.

They are caught in wiers, which are formed by damming up the river, except a space of three or four feet in the middle, which the salmon having passed, are caught in a small inclosure, formed by stakes of wood; the entrance is wide, and gradually lessens, so as barely to admit a single salmon at a time. Every morning, during the fishery, they are taken out, by means of a staff, with a strong

25

barbed iron hook, which is struck into them. But at Ballyshannon, by far the greater number is caught in nets below the fall; they sometimes catch near one hundred at a throw. The time of the fishery is limited; and after it is elapsed, the inclosure is removed, the nets are laid aside, and the fish are at liberty to stock the rivers with spawn. The chief salmon fisheries, besides those in Ireland, are at Berwick on the Tweed, and along the coasts of Scotland. Vast quantities are salted or pickled, and put up in cags, and sent to different parts of the kingdom.

Mrs. HARCOURT.

There are also great quantities of salmon brought fresh to the London markets, by being packed in ice; which, by excluding the air, is found a preservative to many other things. The inhabitants of the northern parts of Europe, the Russians especially, preserve their fowls and other provisions, during their hard winters, when meat is difficult to be procured, in snow and ice.

Mr. HARCOURT.

It would be tedious and unnecessary to particularize the various kinds of fisheries that are in different parts of the world. Oysters, lobsters, pilchards, anchovies, and sturgeon, are all caught in great quantities; the three latter pickled or salted down for use. Cavear, or kavia, a sauce much prized by the Italians, is made of the roe or eggs of the sturgeon. All these form extensive branches of commerce, and supply vast numbers of people with food, who reside at a great distance from the places at which they are caught; at the same time, that they are a means of maintaining thousands of families, by furnishing useful and profitable occupation to them; nor must we omit to mention the great variety and vast numbers of fish, that are eaten without being salted, which daily supply our markets, and provide us with an agreeable change of diet. The produce of the ocean is inexhaustible; nor is it confined to fish alone; the bottom is covered with vegetation in many parts.

AUGUSTA.

How is it possible to know that?

Mr. HARCOURT.

The sea throws up a great variety of sea weeds. Divers also relate that this is the case.

CHARLES.

Can men dive to the bottom of the sea?

Mr. HARCOURT.

There are people who are very expert in diving; but a full account of this curious art is better deferred to another evening, as we have not time to enter into a complete description of the methods of performing it.

SOPHIA.

I have heard that the Giant's Causeway in Ireland is a great natural curiosity; had you an opportunity of seeing it, when you were in that country?

Mr. HARCOURT.

It was an object to which I paid particular attention. It is situated at the northern extremity of the island. It consists of about thirty thousand natural pillars, mostly in a perpendicular situation. At low water the causeway is about six hundred feet long, and probably runs far into the sea, as something familiar is observed on the opposite coast of Scotland. It is not known whether the pillars are continued underground, like a quarry. They are of different dimensions, being from fifteen to twenty-six inches in diameter, and from fifteen to thirty-six feet in height: their figure is generally pentagonal or hexagonal. Several have been found with seven, and a few with three, four, and eight sides, of irregular sizes; every pillar consists as it were of joints or pieces, which are not united by flat surfaces; for on being forced off, one of them is concave in the middle, and the other convex; many of these joints lie loose upon the strand. The stone is a kind of besaltes, of a close grit, and of a dusky hue; it is very heavy, each joint generally weighing two hundred and a half. It clinks like iron, melts in a forge, breaks sharp, and by reason of its extreme hardness, blunts the edges of tools, and by that means is rendered incapable of being used in building. The pillars stand very close to each other, and though the number of their sides differ, yet their contextures are so nicely adapted, as to leave no vacuity between them, and every pillar retains its own thickness, angles, and sides, from top to bottom. These kinds of columns are continued, with interruptions, for near two miles along the shore. By its magnitude and unusual appearance, it

27

forms altogether an object of great rarity, and is mostly visited by all strangers, who have any curiosity.

Mrs. HARCOURT.

This is a wonderful account. It seems to be one of those productions of nature that may be termed an unique. I know of nothing similiar to it. I met with a passage, last night, in Collinson's History of Somerset, though not immediately referring to the subject before us, that I cannot resist the pleasure of repeating. It is concerning a peculiar property of the limpet (a species of shell-fish,) that is found at Minehead in that county; that contains a liquor curious for making linen. When the shell is picked off, there will appear a white vein lying transversely in a little burrow next the head of the fish, which may be taken out by a bodkin, or any other pointed instrument. The letters or figures made with this liquor will presently appear of a light green colour, and if placed in the sun, will change into the following colours; if in winter, about noon; if in summer, an hour or two after sun-rising; and so much before setting; for in the heat of the day in summer, it will come on so fast, that the succession of each colour will scarcely be distinguished. Next to the first light green, it will appear of a deep green, and in a few minutes change to a full sea green; after which, in a few minutes more, it will alter to a blue, then to a purplish red: after which, lying an hour or two, (if the sun shines) it will be of a deep purple red, beyond which the sun does no more. But this last beautiful colour, after washing in scalding water and soap, will, on being laid out to dry, be a fair bright crimson, which will abide all future washing. This species of limpets are, some red, others white, black, yellow, brown, and sand colour, and some are striped with white and brown parallel lines.

SOPHIA.

I should like to have a specimen of this marking liquor. It must be the most elegant of all methods of imprinting letters &c. on linen.

Mrs. HARCOURT.

I believe I have trespassed upon your father's time by this account, but I was much pleased with it. Cecilia, close this conversation, by reciting Mr. Keate's Address to the Ocean.

ADDRESS TO THE OCEAN.*

CECILIA.

"Hail! thou inexhaustible source of wonder and contemplation! Hail! thou mutitudinous ocean! whose waves chase one another down like the generations of men, and after a momentary space, are immerged for ever in oblivion! Thy fluctuating waters wash the varied shores of the world, and while they disjoin nations, whom a nearer connection would involve in eternal war, they circulate their arts, and their labours, and give health and plenty to mankind. How glorious! how aweful are the scenes thou displayest! whether we view thee when every wind is hushed; when the morning sun silvers the level line of the horizon; or when the evening track is marked with flaming gold, and thy unrippled bosom reflects the radiance of the over-arching heavens! Or whether we behold thee in thy terrors! when the black tempest sweeps thy swelling billows, and the boiling surge mixes with the clouds! when death rides the storm, and humanity drops a fruitless tear for the toiling mariner, whose heart is sinking with dismay! And yet, mighty Deep! tis thy surface alone we view. Who can penetrate the secrets of thy wide domain! What eye can visit thy immense rocks and caverns, that teem with life and vegetation? or search out the myriads of objects, whose beauties lie scattered over thy dread abyss? The mind staggers with the immensity of her own conceptions; and when she contemplates the flux and reflux of thy tides, which, from the beginning of the world, were never known to err, how does she shrink at the idea of that Divine Power, which originally laid thy foundations so sure, and whose omnipotent voice hath fixed the limits, where thy proud waves shall be stayed!"

---

* George Keate's verse "Address to the Sea" appeared in his *Sketches from Nature Taken and Coloured in a Journey to Margate* (1779), and was widely reprinted in contemporary magazines.

CONVERSATION 5

HENRY.

I HAVE been thinking, dear papa, that if there were as many whales as herrings, the sea would be hardly large enough to hold them.

Mr. HARCOURT.

Providence has wisely limited the fruitfulness of the larger animals, both on land and in the sea, to a small number: whales, lions, and eagles seldom bring forth more than two at a time. We may also observe with thankfulness, that the increase of noxious animals is generally restricted by the same wise law of nature; whilst those creatures, which are useful to man, multiply very fast. Did the birds and beasts of prey, and huge serpents, increase as fast as domestic animals, this globe would be no longer habitable; we should be forced to resign our places to them, and they would become lords of the creation.

Mrs. HARCOURT.

Your observation ought to excite in us a lively gratitude for the wise arrangement and proportion of creatures in the universe; a striking proof of the wisdom and goodness that governs all things. I have been frequently astonished at the accounts I have read of the increase of fish. There have been found in one cod-fish, 3,686,760 eggs; now, supposing only half, or even a quarter of these eggs to come to perfection, the increase is prodigious. Other kinds of fish multiply also in a surprising degree; yet there is no reason to think that any one kind increases beyond its due proportion with the rest. According to what we remark among the animals, that we have an opportunity of observing, each has its enemy; and it is reasonable to suppose that the same law prevails in the sea; and that each kind has a powerful adversary that diminishes its numbers, and keeps them within due limits.

SOPHIA.

Who could have the patience and perseverance to count such a vast number of small eggs?

Mrs. HARCOURT.

Many naturalists have taken great pains to investigate this curious subject; but Mr. Harmer has pursued it with more success than any of them, by an ingenious method of first weighing the whole spawn very exactly, he then separated a certain number of grains, and carefully counted the number of eggs they contained, by which number he multiplied the remaining grains; thus, by the advantage of method and regularity, he obtained the knowledge of a curious fact in nature easily, in comparison of the trouble he must have taken, to have ascertained it by the tedious method of counting the whole.

CECILIA.

Now I am convinced of what you have often told me, that nothing can be well done without order and method. I will endeavour to be more attentive to this point, and do every thing with greater regularity for the future.

Mrs. HARCOURT.

Order is, indeed, the best guide in every kind of business, and distinguishes a well taught mind, from one that is uninstructed. It should extend to all our concerns; the disposal of our time and money, the proportion of amusement and business should be regulated by some rule, and not left to the direction of mere chance, as is too often the case with many thoughtless people.

CHARLES.

What a prodigious quantity of salt must be consumed in the curing of such multitudes of fish! I am ashamed to confess that I am ignorant whether salt be a natural or an artificial substance.

Mr. HARCOURT.

I will give some account of the manner of its production: you could hardly have chosen a more entertaining subject for our evening's conversation. Common salt, used for seasoning and preserving meat, fish, &c. is one of the most useful necessaries of life; and is of three kinds, viz. fossile or rock salt; sea or marine salt; and spring salt. Fossile or rock salt is found in large beds, or strata, within the bowels of the earth, sometimes crystallized, but more frequently in irregular masses of red, yellow, or blue colour.

HENRY.

Coloured salt! I have never seen any of that kind, why do we not use it?

Mr. HARCOURT.

All salt becomes white by grinding. There are mines of rock-salt in various parts of the world; they are found in Poland, Hungary, Germany, Italy, Spain, and England; as well as in some other countries in Europe. I shall confine myself to describe the manner of procuring this kind of salt, before I say any thing of the other sorts. The account of the Polish mines, in the village of Wiliska, five leagues from Cracow, the capital of Poland, which were discovered in the year 1251, will furnish us with an idea of them, that will serve for a description of salt-mines in general. Their depth and capacity are enterprising. Within them exists a kind of subterraneous republic, or commonwealth, which has its policy, laws, families, &c. nay, even public roads, for horses and carriages, are kept here, for the purpose of drawing the salt to the mouth of the quarry, where it is taken up by engines. These horses, when they are once down, never see the light again; but the men take frequent occasions of breathing the fresh air. What astonishment must a traveller feel, on arriving at the bottom of this wonderful abyss, where so many people are interred alive, and numbers of them even born there, that have never seen day-light. The first thing that strikes him with surprize, is a long series of vaults, sustained by huge pilasters, cut with the chisel out of the rock salt, resembling so many crystals, or precious stones of various colours, reflecting a lustre from the light of the flambeaux, which are continually burning, that dazzles the eye with its splendour; nor can he be less surprised at observing a clear rivulet of fresh water running through the midst of these mountains of salt, and supplying the inhabitants with a source of comfort and accommodation, little to be expected in such a dreary region. The workmen he will find employed in hewing the rocks of salt, in form of huge cylinders, using hammers, pick-axes, and chissels, much as in our stone quarries, in order to separate the several banks. As soon as the massive pieces are got out of the quarry, they break them into fragments proper to be thrown into the mill, where they are ground, and reduced into a coarse farina or flour, which serves all the purposes of sea-salt.

32

CHARLES.

I remember going once with you into a stone quarry, and can therefore easily form an idea of it; but I am surprised to hear that salt is so hard as to require hammers and pick-axes to separate it.

Mr. HARCOURT.

In its natural state, the masses of rock salt are very hard; there are two kinds of sal gemma found in the salt mines of Wiliska; the one harder, and more transparent, and the crystallization of which appears more perfect than that of the other; this the sal gemma of the druggists and dyers. It cuts like crystal, and is frequently used for toys, chaplets, little vases, &c. I think I must procure you some specimens of them, Sophia; they will deserve a place in your cabinet of natural rarities.

SOPHIA.

I shall value them very highly, both as your gift, and as a great curiosity.

Mr. HARCOURT.

The other kind is less compact, and suitable only for kitchen uses. The colour of the salt, while in the mass, is a little brownish; and yet, when ground, it becomes as white as if it had been refined. Some of these masses are found as hard and transparent as crystal; some white, yellow, blue, and fit for various works of taste, in which they engrave as on precious stones. The mine is cold and moist, which causes some difficulty in reducing the salt into powder. They make a blackish salt of the water drawn out of it, which serves to fatten cattle. The salt mines of Catalonia are found in the mountains of the Duchy of Cordona; they form a solid mountain of rock salt, between four and five hundred feet in height, and a league in circumference, and descending to an unknown depth below the surface. This prodigious mountain of salt, which has no mixture of other matter with it, is esteemed a great natural curiosity, and has raised a doubt among naturalists, whether salt does not vegetate or grow. To give you an imperfect idea of the quantities of salt produced annually, it is said, that one of the Northwich pits, which is in Cheshire, has yielded, at a medium, four thousand tons of salt in a year. This salt is esteemed unfit for domestic uses, in its natural state; and therefore they use the method practised in Poland, Hungary, and many other places, on the coarser rock salt;

they refine it, by dissolving it in weak brine and then boiling it into salt again. The works, where the rock salt is refined, are called Refineries. The rock salt is broken small, and put into leaded cisterns, where it is dissolved in cold sea-water, when the solution has stood a day and night to settle, it is drawn off from the sediment into the salt-pan, and refined into salt in the same manner that common salt is boiled up. The scratch, or calcareous matter falling from it, forms a crust on the sides of the cistern. They are careful not to waste the brine left in the pans after the salt is taken out, but add it to the next quantity put into the pan, and so on to the end of the works. I cannot dismiss the subject of rock salt, without mentioning the island of Toongming, in the East Indies, which affords the most remarkable kind of fossile, or native dry salt, in the world. The country is, in general, very fruitful, but in certain parts of the island there are spots of ground, of several acres, which appear wholly barren, yielding not the least appearance of any thing vegetable on them. These spots of ground taste very salt, and abound with salt in such a manner, as not only to supply the whole island, but a great part of the neighbouring continent.

AUGUSTA.

Have the people in this country no other mark to find out the places that produce the salt, than the barrenness of the spot?

Mr. HARCOURT.

When the inhabitants perceive the ground become dry, and covered with white spangles, which are pieces of salt, they are sufficiently assured that this is a proper place to dig for that commodity. It is very remarkable that the same pieces of land, which produce vegetables one year, will produce this salt another; and on the contrary, the salt parts will, some seasons, be covered with vegetation. The salt work in this island is of great advantage to the inhabitants, and supplies all the poor, during the season, with employment. The men are occupied in collecting the salt and wetting the earth, and the women in boiling up the water, which they attend as carefully as the men. The second kind of salt is marine or sea-salt, which is made from sea-water, thickened by repeated evaporation, and at length crystallized.

HENRY.

I do not understand what evaporation means.

Mr. HARCOURT.

Heat, caused either by the action of the sun or fire, makes the watery particles of sea-water fly off, or disperse into the air, and leave the saline parts at the bottom of the vessel, which is called evaporation. The salt, thus deprived of the water, crystallizes, or hardens, and shoots into crystals, such as I shewed you the other day in the microscope. Opaque stones, pyrites, and minerals, when regularly formed, are said to be crystallized; as well as transparent stones and salts. Ice will give you the idea of a complete crystallization, composed of long needle-like masses, flattened on one side, and joined together in such a manner, that the smaller are inserted into the sides of the greater. The crystals of different kinds of salts afford great variety and beauty of forms, and are curious objects of microscopic observation. The regularity of their figure, each different substance producing a form appropriate to itself, is a confirmation, that not only the more obvious works of nature, but also the internal structure of organized bodies, are formed with the same harmony, order, and beauty, that characterize the other parts of the creation. Marine salt is prepared by boiling sea-water. The salt-works are erected near the sea, in order to afford an opportunity of conveying the salt-water into them by pipes, which is afterwards boiled in pans of an immense size. It is necessary to have the roofs of wood fastened with wooden pegs, as the effluvia, which evaporates from the boiling pans, rusts, and destroys iron in a very little time. Whilst boiling, they purify it with whites of eggs, or sometimes the blood of sheep or oxen is used for the same purpose. The saline liquor which remains from the making of salt, is called bittern, and is used for medicinal purposes.

Mrs. HARCOURT.

I think we may observe in the process of salt, as well as many other things, that nature provides materials for man's ingenuity and industry to work upon; nay, she supplies us with few things, that does not require some labour to render them suitable for our use.

Mr. HARCOURT.

Nature has not only furnished us with materials to work with, but implanted in our minds such activity of disposition, and thirst of knowledge, as impels us to scrutinize the properties of these materials, and apply them to the purposes of life. Much has already been discovered, more perhaps lies still behind; the field is vast, and may supply useful and interesting occupation for many succeeding generations of men. The third, and last kind of salt, is prepared in much the same manner as marine salt, from the water of salt wells and springs, and is called brine, or fountain salt. The whitest, driest, and finest grained salt is sometimes made up in form of sugar loaves, in small wicker baskets. In preparing basket salt, they use resin, and other additions, to break the grain, and render it very small; and, to finish the process, it is dried in stoves. Great quantities of brine or spring salt are made in most of the inland countries, as in Germany, Switzerland, Hungary, and in some parts of France and England. Lakes of this kind are found in the Podolian desert, near the river Borysthenes; on the Russian frontiers, towards Crim Tartary; in the kingdom of Algiers; and in other countries. Where nature does not supply these lakes or ponds, artificial ones may be made. This is annually done very advantageously in France, where the chief coasts for bay-salt are those of Bretagne, Saintonge, and the Pay d'Aunis. In order to make a saline, or salt-marsh, a low plot of ground must be chosen adjoining to the sea, and distant from the mouths of large rivers; and to render it complete, it should be near some convenient harbour for vessels. The ground thus chosen, must be hollowed out to three ponds or receptacles. The first, into which the sea-water is admitted, may be called the reservoir; the second receptacle, which is to be again divided into three distinct ponds, communicating with each other by narrow passages, and containing brine of different degrees of strength, may be called the brine-ponds; and the third receptacle, is to be furnished with an entrance, between which and the brine-ponds, there is to run a long narrow winding channel, the rest of it is to be divided into small pits, containing a very strongly saturated brine, which is to be converted into salt, and they may therefore properly be called the salt-pits. The first receptacle must communicate with the sea, by a ditch, defended by walls; the ditch should have a flood-gate to admit , retain, or let out the sea-water, as occasion may require. The bottoms of the reservoir, or brine-ponds, are to be lined with any kind of tough clay, or earth, that will hold water. The proper season for making salt in these artificial salinae, is from May to the end of August. When the salt-men open the flood-gate, at the time the tide is out, to drain off all the stagnating water, and after repairing and cleansing the receptacles from mud and dirt, they admit the sea-water, at the next high tide, till it floats the whole marsh and stands at a proper height in the reservoir. In a few days, most of the water, in the salt-pits, is exaled by the power of the sun, and what remains is a very strong brine. They daily supply themselves with more salt-water, in proportion to what is exhaled by the sun, and the workmen draw out the crystals or salt, as they are formed every day, and dispose them in a pyramidal heap, which they cover over at the top with thatch or straw, to preserve it from the injuries of the weather. Thus, at a small expense and trouble, a salt is prepared, very fit for all domestic uses; and France, especially, is furnished with a very profitable article for exportation. The uses of common salt are various and extensive. Its acid and alkali are employed in many chemical operations in the arts. It is an important ingredient in the fusion of glass, which it whitens and purifies. It facilitates the fusion of the metallic parts of minerals; and its peculiar use in preserving meat, &c. and giving a poignancy to the taste of various kinds of food, is universally known. Common salt is also useful as a manure, by contributing to fertilize the soil.

CHARLES.

You surprise me! I remember to have read in history, of princes, who commanded the lands of their enemies to be sowed with salt, that nothing might grow on them. The Bible furnishes me with an instance of it, when Abimelech destroyed the city of Shechem, he ordered the place where it had stood, to be sowed with salt.

Mr. HARCOURT.

It pleases me to observe, that you remember what you read, and that you apply it as occasion offers. Perhaps the error and prejudice of the ancients arose from this cause, that they were ignorant that though the salt is injurious, and destructive to all vegetables, yet it increases the fertility and productive qualities of the earth.

Mrs. HARCOURT.

That is a very curious distinction, that I was unacquainted with before. It grows late; our lecture has been rather long this evening.

Mr. HARCOURT.

It is time to separate, and as I have related the most important particulars concerning salt, and the manner of preparing it, we will withdraw. Good night, children.

CONVERSATION 6

AUGUSTA.

SOME gentlemen dined with us to-day, who came from Canada, in North-America. I believe they took me for an ignorant girl, that might easily be made to believe any thing. I assure you, they quite vexed me; they told me a number of improbable stories of an animal, that builds houses three stories high, makes bridges, and I know not what ridiculous stuff. I hate to be imposed upon, so I left the table as soon as the cloth was removed, and hastened here to tell you how I have been served.

Mrs. HARCOURT.

Sophia, what is the name of this extraordinary animal, that has caused so much offence to Augusta?

SOPHIA.

I suppose it was the beaver, mamma.

AUGUSTA.

Ay, that is the very name; but I cannot believe these accounts to be true.

Mrs. HARCOURT.

Sophia studies natural history, she shall give us the particulars with which she is acquainted, concerning this curious creature.

Mr. HARCOURT.

Charles has been this morning to inspect a hat manufactory, and is therefore prepared to complete his sister's account of the beaver, by informing us what use is made of its fur. Sophia, it is your turn to begin.

SOPHIA.

Beaver or Castor, makes a distinct genus of animals of the order of *Glires*, and class of *Mammalia*. The characters are, that the upper fore teeth are truncated, and hollowed obliquely, and that the lower are oblique at the apex; with a flat tail, and feet which have five toes on each, and palms adapted to swimming. Under this genus are comprehended three species. The Beaver or Fiber. Secondly, the Castor. Thirdly, the Castor, called *Zibethicus*.

Mr. HARCOURT.

Very well defined, with the method and precision of a naturalist. Give us now a description of the animal, and afterwards, its manner of living and habits.

SOPHIA.

The beaver is about four feet in length, and twelve or fifteen inches broad; his skin in the northern regions is generally black; but it brightens into a reddish hue, in the temperate climates. He is covered with two sorts of hair, one long, and the other a soft down; the latter, which is an inch in length, is extremely fine and compact, and furnishes the animal with a necessary degree of warmth, the long hair preserves the down from dirt and wet. The head is like that of the otter, but longer, the snout is pretty long, the eyes small, the ears short, round and hairy on the outside, but smooth within, and the teeth very long, the under teeth project the breadth of three fingers, and the upper, half a finger, all of which are broad, crooked, strong, and sharp; besides those teeth, which are called incisors, which grow double, are set very deep in their jaws, and bend like the edge of an axe; they have sixteen grinders, eight on each side, four above, and four below, directly opposite to each other. With the former, they are able to cut down trees of a considerable size; with the latter, to bring the hardest substances; the legs are short, the fore-legs not exceeding four or five inches in length, the fore-paws are formed something like the human hand. These feet serve the beaver to dig, soften, and work the clay for different purposes, the hind feet are furnished with membranes, or large skins, extending between the toes, like those of ducks, and other water-fowl; the tail is long, a little flat, entirely covered with scales, supplied with muscles, and perpetually moistened with oil or fat, which the creature distributes all over them with his snout, and which he procures from four bags, which are placed under the intestines, and are found in every beaver, whether male or female. These bags are filled with a resinous liquid substance, which, when it is ejected, settles into a thick consistence. Physicians call it castoreum, and prescribe it as an excellent remedy against poisons, vapours, and other maladies, but when it grows old, it blackens, and degenerates into a dangerous poison.

Mrs. HARCOURT.

Before Sophia relates the manners and occupations of this creature, let us give particular attention to the implements with which nature has furnished it. The form and strength of the teeth are suited to cutting of wood and hard substances, and we have already been told that with these they are able to fell trees; the fore-paws are adapted to handling and disposing the materials of the work; the hind-feet are formed for swimming, and evidently shew that the creature is intended to live in both elements, and is what is called an amphibious animal; the tail, from its flatness, and the hardness of its scales, may serve very well for a hod, such as bricklayers use for carrying mortar, &c. And now, Augusta, do you think it totally improbable, that a creature furnished with such tools, and endued with a proportionable degree of sagicity to use them, should be able to construct houses of three stories, or build bridges, &c.

AUGUSTA.

Indeed I begin to be staggered; but is this really the case? Pray, Sophia, go on, for I am impatient to hear what you have to tell us further on this subject.

SOPHIA.

When they are going to chuse a place to build a habitation, they assemble in companies sometimes of two or three hundred, and after mature deliberation, fix on a spot where plenty of provisions, and all necessaries may be found. Their houses are always situated in the water; and when they can find neither lake nor pond adjacent, they endeavour to supply the defect, by stopping the current of some brook or small river, by means of a causey or dam; for this purpose they set about felling of trees, which several of them together effect pretty easily, with their strong teeth; they take care to chuse out those that grow above the place where they intend to build, that they may swim down the current. They also, with wonderful sagacity, contrive that they shall fall towards the water, that they may have the less way to carry them. After the tree is felled, they cut it into proper lengths, and then roll them into the water, and navigate them towards the place where they are to be used. The causey raised with these pieces of wood, is sometimes ten or a dozen feet in thickness at the foundation; it descends in a slope on the side next the water. The opposite side is raised perpendicularly like our walls, and the slope, which at its base is twelve feet broad, diminishes towards the top to the breadth of two feet. They drive the extremities of these pieces of wood very near each other, into the earth, and interlace them with other stakes more slender and supple. But as the water, without some other prevention, would glide through the cavities, and leave the reservoir dry, they have recourse to a clay, which they perfectly well know how to procure, and which they work up into a kind of mortar with their tails, and close up the interstices with it, both within and without, and this entirely secures the water from passing away. If the violence of the water, or the footsteps of hunters, who pass over their work, damage it, they immediately set about repairing it. They build their cabins, either on piles in the middle of the small lakes, they have thus formed, on the bank of a river, or at the extremity of some point of land, that advances into a lake. The figure of them is round or oval, divided into three partitions, raised one above another. The first is sunk below the level of the dike, and is generally full of water, the other two stories are built over it. The whole edifice is mostly capable of containing eight or ten inhabitants. Each beaver has its peculiar cell assigned him, the floor of which he strews with leaves, or small branches of the pine-tree, so as to render it clean and comfortable. Their works, especially in the cold regions, are completed in August or September; after which they furnish themselves with a store of provisions. During the summer, they regale upon all the fruits and plants the country produces. In the winter they eat the wood of the ash, the plane, and other trees, which they steep in water, in quantities proportionable to their consumption, and they are supplied with a double stomach, to facilitate the digestion of such solid food, at two operations. They cut twigs from three to six feet in length, the larger ones are conveyed by several beavers to the magazine, and the smaller by a single animal, but they take different ways. Each individual has his walk assigned him, to prevent the labourers from being interrupted in their respective occupations. These parcels of wood are not piled up in one continued heap, but laid across one another with interstices between them that they may the easier draw out what quantity they want; and they always take the parcel at the bottom. They cut this wood into small pieces, and convey it to their cell, where the whole family come to receive their share. Sometimes they wander in the woods, and regale their young with a fresh collation. The hunters, who know that these creatures love green wood better than old, place a parcel of the former about their lodge, and then have several devices to ensnare them. When the

41

winter grows severe, they sometimes break the ice, and when the beavers come to the opening for air, they kill them with hatchets, or make a large aperture in the ice, and cover it with a very strong net, and then overturn the lodge, upon which the beavers, thinking to escape in their usual way, by flying to the water, and immerging at the hole in the ice, fall into the snare, and are taken.

CECILIA.

Poor creatures! what can induce anybody to be so cruel, as to ensnare and destroy such ingenious and industrious animals?

Mr. HARCOURT.

Profit. The hunters in America catch vast numbers of them every year, for the sake of their skins, and bags of castor, which they bring to the merchants, who send them to Europe.

CECILIA.

Pray what use do they make of their skins?

Mr. HARCOURT.

I leave Charles to answer that question.

CHARLES.

Men's hats are made of the fur of the Beaver. Women are employed by the hatters, to clear the skins of the hair; for which purpose they use two knives; a large one, like a shoe-maker's knife, for the long hair; and a smaller, not unlike a vine knife, to shave or scrape off the short hair or down. When the hair is off, they mix the stuff, putting to one third of dry caster, two thirds of old coat, a term they use for the hair of those skins which have been worn some time by the savages, and by what means is become finer than the rest. After it is mixed, they card it; which is pulling it smooth and even, between two things resembling a curry comb, with fine teeth: such as are used to card wool with, before it is spun. They then take a proper quantity of this stuff for a hat, and put it upon the hurdle, which is a square table with chinks cut through it lengthwise, then the workman takes an instrument, called a bow, very like a fiddle-stick, and works the fur till it mixes well together, the dirt and filth passing through the chinks. In this manner they form two gores or pieces of an oval form, ending in a sharp corner at top. These pieces, or capades, as they are called, being formed

42

in this manner, they proceed to harden them in closer and more consistent flakes, by pressing them with a hardening skin or leather; they are then carried to the bason, which is a sort of bench, with an iron plate fitted in it, and a little fire underneath it, upon which they lay one of the capades, sprinkled with water, and make use of a sort of mould to form it; when, by means of the heat of the fire, the water, and pressing, the substance thickens into a slight hairy sort of felt or stuff. After they have turned up the edges all round the mould, they lay it by, and proceed in the same manner with the other half. The next thing is to join the two pieces together, so as to meet in a point at the top, and form a high crowned cap. The hat thus basoned, is removed to a large receiver or trough, which is a kind of copper kettle, of peculiar shape, filled with hot water and grounds, after dipping the hat in the kettle they begin to work it, by rolling and unrolling it again and again, first with their hands, and then with a little wooden roller, dipping it frequently in the kettle, till by fulling and thickening it in this manner for four or five hours, it is brought into the size of the hat intended; they form the crown by laying the high crowned cap on a wooden block of a proper size, and tying it round with a packthread, called a commander, which they gradually push down to the bottom of the block, with a piece of iron properly bent, which they call a stamper. When the hat is dried, they singe it, and rub it with pumice, to take off the coarser knap, it is afterwards rubbed with seal-skin, and lastly carded with a fine card.

Mr. HARCOURT.

You have given us a very clear account of what you saw this morning; but pray tell us, whether something is not to be done to colour and stiffen the hat.

CHARLES.

O yes! the hat is sent upon the block of the dyer's, who makes a dye of log-wood, verdegrease, copperas, and aster-bark, and fills his copper with it, which is mostly large enough to hold ten or twelve dozen of hats at a time. He boils the hats in this dye for near an hour, then sets them out to cool, and boils them again ten or more times over, till the dye is complete; it is now returned to the hatter, who dries it thoroughly over a charcoal fire, and then smears it with glue, or gum senegal dissolved, to stiffen it. The next thing is to steam it on the steaming bason, which is a little hearth or fire-place, covered over with an iron plate that exactly fits it; on

43

this plate wet cloths are spread, to prevent the hat from burning, the hat is placed brim downwards on it, and rubbed gently with the hand, till sufficiently steamed, and dried; it is then put again upon the block, and brushed and ironed with flat-irons, such as are used for ironing linen, which smoothens and polishes it, and nothing now remains to be done, but to clip the edges, and sew a lining into the crown.

Mrs. HARCOURT.

I thank you in the name of the company for the entertainment you have given us, and cannot help observing the wisdom of Providence, that has so wonderfully suited the formation and instincts of the beaver to its wants, and appointed manner of life.

AUGUSTA.

I am all astonishment and wonder; and for the future, shall be more ready to listen to extraordinary things with attention; but I thought it foolish to give credit to any thing that seemed so improbable.

Mrs. HARCOURT.

There is a material difference between credulously assenting to every thing we hear without examination; and listening attentively to the relations of people of sense and credit, who have no motive for imposing upon us; and who, if we have patience, will probably give good reasons for what they assert; but it is a mark of ignorance to believe every thing implicitly. Much depends upon the degree of credit due to the character of the person who relates the circumstance; but there are such wonders in both nature and art, that till they are explained, may well appear improbable to the uninformed mind; this reflection should incite us to pursue the attainment of useful knowledge, by attending to the conversation of people of experience and information.

Mr. HARCOURT.

Conversation is an agreeable means of instruction: and those people, who by a habit of attention and observation, collect knowledge wherever it is to be found, may meet with it from the most clownish rustic or unlettered mechanic. Never despise any body as too mean to learn from; but talk to every one in his own way;

that is, on the subject of his profession or calling, and you may with certainty rely upon gaining information.

Mrs. HARCOURT.

We have passed the time so pleasantly, that we have not been aware how late it is; it is time to take leave. Children, good night.

CONVERSATION 7

Mrs. HARCOURT.

BUSINESS prevents your father from his usual attendance, therefore we must find something to entertain ourselves with; cannot we contrive some game or play to amuse us?

SOPHIA.

If you please, mamma, we will play at questions, in the manner Miss Groves shewed us. You must propose a question, which each of us must try to answer in turn. Whoever gives a proper reply gains a prize.

CECILIA.

What shall the prizes be?

CHARLES.

They need not be of any great value, some trifle for the sake of the play.

Mrs. HARCOURT.

I received a present yesterday, of some shells and fossile productions, it will give me pleasure to distribute them along you; they will just suit the purpose. Sophia, you will find them in my cabinet: bring them, and dispose them in equal parcels.

SOPHIA.

What beautiful tints! What colours can equal these? Shells, flowers, and insects are the finishings of nature, and for elegance of form, variety, and beauty of colour, as well as delicacy of texture, excel the finest works of art.

Mrs. HARCOURT.

They will serve two purposes. The one as prizes for your answers, the other as a subject for my first question. What is a shell?

HENRY.

A shell is a house for a snail or a small fish to live in.

46

Mrs. HARCOURT.

A prize belongs to Henry for his answer, as it is certain that shells furnish a case or covering, or if you please a habitation for the insects that dwell in them; They also serve them as a defence, or coat of mail against their enemies, or any thing that might injure their tender bodies; but I mean to enquire in what manner the shell is produced.

CECILIA.

I suppose it is a part of the animal, formed with it as bones are.

Mrs. HARCOURT.

That was thought to be the case formerly, but the discoveries of M. Reaumur has shewn the supposition to be false; he has proved that the shells of snails are formed from the perspiration of the animal, which is concreted or hardened by the air; and it is reasonable to suppose that the sea-water has the same effect on those of fishes. The casting of the shell of crabs and lobsters tends to confirm this opinion.

AUGUSTA.

Do they ever change their shells?

Mrs. HARCOURT.

Yes, my dear, every year. The creature, aware of what it has to undergo, retreats to a place of security, such as the cavities of rocks, or under great stones, where it lies till all the parts are by degrees disengaged from the old shell. In this naked state they make a very disagreeable appearance, being a mere lump of flesh covered with a sort of jelly, which by degrees hardens into a shell, somewhat larger than the old one, and thus accommodates itself to the growth of the animal.

CHARLES.

This is very wonderful indeed; are shells a perfect defence to the fish that live in them?

Mrs. HARCOURT.

I propose that as my next question, to be answered by the company.

47

SOPHIA.

I suppose there is no manner of doubt, as mamma has already told us, that they defend the fish against many injuries; but I read a little while ago, that they are not a perfect security against all. Shell-fish are the food of some fish of the larger kinds, particularly the sea-porcupine, and a species of the wray-fish, feed chiefly upon them. These fish are provided by nature with a suitable apparatus for grinding them into a state proper for digestion, their jaws being furnished with bony substances extending to the palate, and under part of the mouth, which are capable of reducing strong shells into a pulp; but what is most extraordinary is, that a small pectunculus or cockle, is the prey of the soal, which has no such instruments for breaking them to pieces, but is supposed to be furnished with a menstruum in the body, that has the power of dissolving them; for on examining the inside of a soal, many of these shells are found in part dissolved, whilst others remain unaltered.

Mrs. HARCOURT.

How various are the powers of nature, she is not obliged to perform the same thing always by the same means, but uses variety of processes to produce the same effect. Into how many classes are shells divided by the best naturalists?

CHARLES.

A visit to the British Museum, in company with a friend of my papa's, who is a collector of shells, has rendered me capable of resolving that question; they are generally divided into three classes. Univalves, bivalves, and multivalves; which include sea, land, and fresh water shells, which are subdivided into many genera and species. The first class consists of shells that are of one single piece, as a snail-shell; the second, of those which are formed of two, as the oyster or muscle; and the third, of those which have more pieces than two. Sea-eggs will afford us an example of these, being covered with spines or prickles. Land-shells are of two kinds, the recent and the fossile; the recent are those which are inhabited by living animals; but the fossile are the remains of marine bodies, supposed to have once inhabited the deep seas, though frequently found in great quantities under ground, in mines, and in places far distant from the ocean, and sometimes on the tops of mountains.

AUGUSTA.

Astonishing! by what strange accident could they ever come there?

CHARLES.

That question has puzzled many wise and learned men; it is generally believed that those parts have many ages ago been covered with sea, and some refer to the grand deluge as the cause of this wonderful change; they are very advantageous to the places where they are found, as they afford an excellent manure for land.

SOPHIA.

This is a convincing proof of the truth of the history of the deluge: the account that Moses gives us of the flood has always appeared to me so wonderful, that I could scarcely believe it; but I think, after this confirmation, I shall never doubt again concerning any thing, however extraordinary that I find written in the Scriptures.

Mrs. HARCOURT.

Remember, my dear, that the sacred writings contain a history of the miraculous interposition of divine Providence, in teaching mankind the most holy and pure religion, from the earliest ages to the glorious dispensation of the Gospel. Can we then be surprised, that they should contain things out of the course of nature? the very essence of a miracle is, that an effect is produced which can only be accounted for by the influence of a supernatural power. In the rude ages of gross ignorance, when the worship of idols was almost universal, some striking instances of a miraculous display of divine power was necessary to convince men, that a God existed, who had created all things, and who governed them with an all-seeing eye. The children of Israel were chosen as a peculiar people, among whom were displayed these extraordinary manifestations of the divine Preference, that by their means the worship of the One True God might supplant the adoration paid to the sun, moon, stars, animals of various kinds, and even to stocks and stones, by the different nations of the earth. The multitude of fossil bodies found in places remote from the sea are an incontrovertible proof of some violent convulsion of nature and perhaps are permitted to remain as a monument, to silence all cavillers on the subject; but let us resume the thread of our discourse: the vast variety of shells that are seen in the cabinets of collectors are not all the produce of one sea or one country. Some of the most beautiful come from the East-Indies and the Red-Sea. The colours and brilliancy of shells seem to be improved and heightened by the heat of the sun, as those of warm climates always excel those found in cold countries in lustre. The shores of Asia furnish us with the pearl-oysters and scallops in great perfection. Shells of great beauty are also found on the shores of America and the West-Indies. In Africa, on the coast of Guinea, abounds a small species of porcelain shells, which the natives use as money.

AUGUSTA.

I thought nothing could serve the purpose of money but gold and silver.

Mrs. HARCOURT.

Gold and silver are only used as a representation of real wealth. I give you a certain quantity of gold, in exchange for which you supply me with corn, cattle, or any of the necessaries of life. With the gold that you have received, you purchase some other commodity that you want from a third person, who likewise barters it in the same manner for something that he stands in need of; thus it passes from one to another, enabling them to exchange the commodities of life in a more exact proportion, with respect to the value of each, than could be done without such a medium. Shells, or any other durable substance, may answer the same purpose as gold, if men agree to receive it in the same way. The women of this country adorn their hair, and make bracelets and necklaces with another kind, which are perfectly white.

HENRY.

How droll they must look upon their black faces and necks.

SOPHIA.

We have different ideas of beauty, Henry; perhaps they are as well satisfied with these simple ornaments, as our women of fashion are with diamonds and rouge: but we interrupt mamma.

Mrs. HARCOURT.

The Mediterranean and Northern Ocean contain great variety of shells, and many of remarkable elegance and beauty; but upon the whole they are greatly inferior to those of the East-Indies. Our own English coasts are not the last in the production of shells, though they cannot be compared to those of the East-Indies for lustre and colour.

CECILIA.

I think I have heard that there is a method of polishing shells, mamma; will you be so kind as to tell us how it is done?

Mrs. HARCOURT.

There are various methods of polishing shells, and adding to their natural beauty. Among the immense variety of shells with which we are acquainted, some are taken out of the sea, or found on its shores, in their utmost perfection, and cannot be improved by the hand of art, their beautiful tints being spread upon the surface, and the natural polish superior to any that could be given: but in others the beauties are concealed by a coarse outer coat, which the hand of a skilful polisher may remove. Collectors should have specimens of the same species, both rough and polished, that the naturalist may compare the natural state with the artificial one. How many fine strokes of nature's pencil in this part of the creation would be entirely concealed from our view, were it not for the assistance of an art that unveils and displays them in full lustre? A shell that has a smooth surface and a natural dull polish, requires only to be rubbed with the hand, or a piece of chamoy, leather, or some tripoli or fine rotten stone may be used, and it will become perfectly, bright and polished; but even this should be done with caution, for in many shells the lines are only on the surface, and the wearing ever so little of the shell defaces it. A shell that is rough, foul, and crusty, or covered with a tartareous coat, must be steeped for some hours in hot water, then it is to be rubbed with rough emery on a stick, in order to get off the coat; after this it may be dipped in diluted aqua-fortis, spirit of salt, or any other acid, and after remaining a few moments in it, be again dipped in common water; then it is to be well rubbed with soap-suds; after which the operation may be finished with fine emery, and, a hair-brush; and many, to heighten the polish, rub the shell with a thin solution of gum arabic, or the white of an egg; gloves should be worn in using the aqua-fortis, as it is liable to injure the flesh wherever it touches. Some shells require more severe treatment, which is called scaling them, and is performed by a horizontal wheel of lead or tin, impregnated with rough emery, and the shell is worked down in

51

the same manner as stones are by the lapidary; this requires the hand of a skilful artist to avoid wearing away the shell too low, and spoiling it. After the shell is cut down as far as is proper, it is to be polished with fine emery, tripoli or rotten stone, with a wooden wheel, turned by the same machine as the leaden one. These are the principal means used in this art, and the changes that are produced by it, are often so great, that the shell is not to be known for the same; for instance, the onyx or volute is of a simple pale brown in its natural state, and becomes a fine bright yellow, with only just the superficies taken off; but if eaten away deeper, appear of a milk-white, with a bluish hue towards the bottom. In the East-Indies they frequently engrave lines, circles, and other devices on many species of shells, particularly the nautilus; but this is a gross violation of good taste; so far from embellishing or heightening the charms of nature, it does not even imitate them.

CHARLES.

When we go to the sea-side, in autumn, we may collect shells, and polish them at our leisure hours. Among other curiosities that were pointed out to my observation, at the British Museum, was a piece of byssus, which is a fine cloth, used by the ancients, when silk was rare, made of the threads of the pinna marina, a fish somewhat like a muscle but much larger, and is held in its place in the same manner, by a prodigious number of very fine threads, which the animal has the power of spinning as it finds occasion, as the spider and caterpillar do. These threads have in all times been used for the same purposes as silk. At present they are manufactured at Palermo, the chief city of Sicily, and other places, into gloves, stockings, and different sorts of wearing apparel. The method of rendering it fit to use, is by laying it for a few days in a damp cellar to soften, then comb and cleanse it; and lastly spin it, in the same manner as they do silk. By these threads, the pinna marina, or sea-wing, as it is sometimes called, suspends itself to the rocks twenty or thirty feet beneath the surface of the sea. In this situation, it is so successfully attacked by the eight-footed polypus, that the species could not exist, but for the assistance of the cancer pinnotheris, which lives in the same shell, as a guard and companion. The pinnotheris or pinnophylax is a small crab, naked like Bernard the hermit, but is furnished with good eyes, and always inhabits the shell of the pinna; when they want food, the pinna opens its shell, and sends its faithful ally to forage; but if the cancer sees the polypus, he returns suddenly to the arms of his blind hostess, who, by closing the shell, avoids the fury of her enemy; otherwise, when it has procured a booty, it brings it to the opening of the shell, where it is admitted, and they divide the prey.

AUGUSTA.

This is curious indeed; that one animal should supply eyes for another, in return for the advantage of a coat of mail.

Mrs. HARCOURT.

It is almost time to distribute the prizes. Henry, that small lot of beautiful shells belongs to you. Charles will take these pieces of coral, and prepare himself by tomorrow evening to give us some account of the nature of coral, whether animal or vegetable; and Sophia, this paper nautilus is reserved for you. I hope you are able to give us some particulars relative to the fish that inhabited it.

SOPHIA.

The general form of the nautilus is adapted to swimming on the water, and resembles the figure of a boat or vessel, but varies in some particulars in the different species. The name is derived from a greek word, signifying both a fish and a sailor. It is supposed that men first took the idea of sailing in vessels from what they saw practised by this little creature. The paper nautilus is so named from the thinness of the shell, which it sometimes creeps out of, and goes on shore to feed. When this animal intends to sail, it extends two of its arms on high, and supports a membrane between them, which it throws out to serve as a sail, and its two other arms hang out of the shell to be used occasionally as oars, or as a steerage; but this last office is generally performed by the tail. When the sea is calm, numbers of these fish are frequently seen diverting themselves with sailing about in this manner, but as soon as a storm arises, or any thing disturbs them they draw in their arms, and take in as much water as makes them a little heavier than the sea-water in which they swim, and by that means sink to the bottom. When they desire to rise again, they expel this abundant water through a number of holes which they have in their arms, and so lighten themselves.

Mrs. HARCOURT.

The manners and instincts of those animals that inhabit the ocean, are greatly concealed from us by their situation, but those few, that have offered themselves to our observation, display instances of the same admirable wisdom that has formed the inhabitants of the earth and air. Should man ever be enabled, by any future discovery to traverse the bottom of the sea, what wonders would be opened to his view! What numberless examples of contrivance and sagacity, directed by the same wisdom, that has instructed the bee to gather honey, and the beaver to construct his habitation, would appear! The different contrivances that several species of fish, whose manners are known, discover, in the modes of catching their prey, are so wonderful and curious, that I cannot deny myself the pleasure of relating a few instances. The sturgeon is without teeth, and his mouth placed under the head, like the opening of a purse, which he has the power of pushing suddenly out, or retracting. Before this mouth, under the beak or nose, hang four tendrils some inches long, and which so resemble earth-worms, that at first sight they may be mistaken for them. This clumsy toothless fish is supposed by this contrivance to keep himself in good condition, the solidity of his flesh evidently shew-ing him to be a fish of prey. He is said to hide his large body amongst the weeds near the sea-coasts, or at the mouths of large rivers, only exposing his irrhi or tendrils, which small fish or sea-insects mistaking for real worms, approach for plunder, and are sucked into the jaws of their enemy. The flesh of the sturgeon was so valued in the the time of the emperor Severus, that it was brought to table by servants with coronets on their heads, and preceded by music, which might give rise to its being in our country presented by the lord mayor to the king. At present it is caught in the Danube and the Wolga, the Don, and other large rivers, for various purposes. The skin makes the best covering for carriages; isinglass is prepared from parts of the skin, cavear from the spawn; and the flesh is pickled or salted, and sent all over Europe, as your father told you in his account of the fisheries. There is a sea insect described by Mr. Huges, whose claws or tentacles being disposed in regular circles, and tinged with a variety of bright lively colours, represent the petals of some most elegantly fringed and radiated flowers; as the carnation, marigold, and anemone; these beautiful rays serve them as a net for inclosing their prey. These entertaining subjects have insensibly led us on till it is late. Good night, children, let us retire.

CONVERSATION 8

Mr. HARCOURT.

GOOD evening to you, ladies, I regretted losing the pleasure of joining your party last night, but understand from Mrs. Harcourt, that you were very well amused with the subject of shells and fossils.

CECILIA.

Nothing was wanting but your company, to render our evening delightful.

Mrs. HARCOURT.

Delightful, my dear Cecilia, that is too strong a word; learn to moderate your expressions, suit your terms to the occasion; or you will be at a loss to raise your language in proportion to your feelings, when important events excite your liveliest emotions.

CECILIA.

How often do I forget your precepts in this respect, although I endeavour to attend to them; but I did enjoy myself so very much last night, that I thought I might say delightful, without any exaggeration.

Mrs. HARCOURT.

I am glad you were so well pleased, but restrain the warmth of your expressions; an excess in this way, may be ranked among the follies of the present fashionable manners; it is not only absurd in itself, but tends to give us false ideas of things, and induces us to consider that as important, which in its own nature is but trifling. Whenever I hear a girl exclaim, upon every little variation of weather, I am dying of heat, I am frozen to death; or melting in ecstacies at a concert or a play, I suspect either that her imagination has been suffered to run wild, or that she has never been instructed to adapt her language to her ideas. Such excess of speech is to be expected from novel and romance readers, but are ill suited to a woman of good sense and propriety of manners. — Well, Charles, we expect our entertainment from you, tonight. Have you been able to discover whether corals and corallines are to be ranked in the vegetable or animal kingdom?

55

CHARLES.

Linnaeus* has classed them among the zoophytes, which are a kind of intermediate body, supposed to partake both of the nature of an animal and a vegetable, as the Greek word from which it is derived, indicates, signifying plant animal. In the Linnaean system, the zoophytes, which constitute the fifth order of worms, are composite animals, resembling flowers and springing from a vegetating stem. This order contains fifteen genera, of which nine are fixed, and have no power of removing from the places where they are formed; as the isis or red coral, sea-fan or gorgonia, alcyonium, sponge, flustra, tubularia, corallines, fertularia, and vorticella; but the others possess the faculty of transporting themselves from one place to another, as the hydra or polype, the pennatula or sea-pen, toenia, volvex, furia, and chaos, or the assemblage of chaotic or microscopical animals. The species under this order are one hundred and fifty-six. The immense and dangerous rocks built by the swarms of coral insects in the Southern Ocean, which rise perpendicularly like walls, are described in Cook's Voyages. A point of one of these rocks broke off, and stuck in the hole that it had made in the bottom of one of his ships, which must otherwise have perished by the admission of water.

Mr. HARCOURT.

Their prodigious multiplication in all ages of the world is shewn by the numerous lime-stone rocks, which consist of a congeries or heap of the cells of these animals, which constitute a great part of the solid earth. Specimens of these rocks are to be seen in the lime-works at Linsel, near Newport, in Shropshire; in Coalbrook Dale; and in several parts of the Peak of Derbyshire. It is remarkable that many of those found in a fossil state, differ from any species of the recent ones that are known, and have either been produced in the deep seas, where no human eye can penetrate, or are become extinct. I suppose, Charles, you can inform us from

---

* The Swedish botanist and taxonomist Carl Linnaeus (1707-78) developed systems for classifying animals and plants, and pioneered in introducing two-word names for animals and plants. In the 10th edition of *Systema Naturae* (1758) he classified all animals as either mammals, birds, amphibians, fish, insects, or "worms" (invertebrates). Linnaeus's classification of plants, the Sexual System, was based upon the reproductive parts of a flower.

what country the best coral comes, and in what manner it is procured.

CHARLES.

The fishing season for coral is from April to July. The places are the Persian Gulf, Red Sea, coasts of Africa, towards the Bastion of France, the isles of Majorca and Corsica, and the coasts of Provence and Catalonia. Seven or eight men go in a boat; the caster throws the net, which is formed of two beams, tied across with a leaden weight to press them down. A great quantity of hemp is loosely twisted round, among which they mix some strong nets and fasten to the beams; thus prepared it is let down into the sea, and when the coral is pretty much entangled, they draw it out by a rope, which sometimes requires half a dozen boats to effect. It is used as a medicine in various diseases.

SOPHIA.

I suppose it is but lately that the real nature of coral has been ascertained; was it not formerly reckoned a vegetable?

Mr. HARCOURT.

It was formerly ranked among the number of marine plants, but the discoveries of modern naturalists have raised it to the animal kingdom, since their observations satisfactorily prove that it is the structure and habitation of certain sea-animals, and designed for their protection and support. The nature and origin of coral have been as much disputed as any subject in natural knowledge. Some have considered coral, and the other similar productions of the sea as stone. They adopted this opinion from their excessive hardness, and specific gravity, as well as from observing that when these bodies were calcined, they were converted into lime. Kircher supposes that there are entire forests of it at the bottom of the sea, which is not at all improbable, since M. de Peysonnel has demonstrated, by his experiments, that it is constructed by an animal of the polype kind. In forming coral, and other marine productions of this class, the animal labours like those of the testaceous kind, each according to its species, and their productions vary according to their several forms, magnitudes, and colours. The coral insect, he observes, expands itself in water and contracts itself in air; or when it is touched with the hand, or when acid liquors are poured upon it; and he actually saw these insects move their claws or legs, and expand themselves when the water in which they were, was placed near the fire. Broken branches of coral have been observed to fasten to other branches. The coral insects, not having been injured, continue their operations, and as they draw no sustenance from the stone of the coral, they are able to increase in a detached state. M. de Peysonnel observed that it grows in every direction, sometimes horizontally, sometimes perpendicularly downwards, at other times upwards. Coral then is a mass of animals of the polyp kind, having the same relation to the polypes united to them, that there is between the shell of a snail, and the snail itself. Pray, Charles, tell us how many kinds of coral there are?

CHARLES.

There are three kinds; red, white, and black; the black is the rarest, and most esteemed; but it is the red that is mostly used in medicine. There is no part of the world where white coral is produced in such abundance as on the shores of the island of Ceylon, and other of the neighbouring coasts. The lime made in those countries for building houses, fortifications, &c. is all prepared by burning this coral. It lies in vast banks, which are uncovered at low water, and it is spongy and porous. While young, it is formed erect in shape of little shrubs, and is then firm and solid, with a smooth surface; but the branches continually shoot out, and from those new branches proceed others, till the whole is one confused bush, which is all covered with a white viscous matter, which in time hardens upon them, and becomes coral; and this filling up all the interstices, and hardening between them, renders it one coarse rock.

CECILIA.

I observed you named sponge among the zoophytes; surely that cannot be the habitation of insects. I have often wondered what it is, but have never been able to satisfy my curiosity.

Mr. HARCOURT.

Sponge is a kind of marine substance found adhering to rocks, shells, &c. under cover of the sea-water. Naturalists have till lately been greatly embarrassed in which of the three kingdoms to place it; but it is now decidedly allowed to be of some species of worm or polype. The same M. de Peysonnel has discovered, and described the worms that form four different species of sponges; he thinks the sponge is formed from the juice or slaver, which is deposited by the worms that inhabit them.

HENRY.

The next time I have any to rub my slate with, I will try if I can find any of these insects.

Mrs. HARCOURT.

It will be a vain endeavour. The insects are all dead, long before the sponge comes to our hands; besides they are so small as to require the best microscopes to discover them.

AUGUSTA.

I know a lady that has a beautiful grotto in her garden ornamented with a variety of corals and shells. I shall observe it with more attention the next time I visit her.

CHARLES.

I wonder any body should bestow the money and trouble, necessary to form such a collection, to place them in a garden, where they are liable to be stolen, and are exposed to the injuries of the weather.

SOPHIA.

Perhaps the corals are artificial, and ordinary shells, mixed with pebbles, and pieces of coloured glass; the refuse of the glass-house, would have a very pretty effect.

CECILIA.

Artificial coral! I never heard of such a thing. Pray, sister, how do they make it?

SOPHIA.

After having chosen twigs and branches to your fancy, resembling the manner of the growth of coral as much as possible; you must peel and dry them. Then take one ounce of clear rosin, and dissolve it in a brass pan, to which add two drams of the finest vermilion, mix these ingredients well together, and paint the branches with it whilst it is warm, then hold them over a gentle coal fire, till they are smooth and even, as if polished. In the same manner, white coral may be imitated with white lead, and black coral with lampblack.

CHARLES.

If papa and mamma will give us leave, we will build one near the river at the top of the grove. I will undertake to be the architect, and perform the rough work.

Mrs. HARCOURT.

I approve the plan, and will assist in the execution of it.

Mr. HARCOURT.

I agree to it, on one condition, that it shall not infringe upon the time of your studies. Rise an hour earlier every morning, that will give you sufficient opportunity for the work.

CECILIA.

That will be no hardship, these beautiful mornings; let us agree to meet at six o'clock.

AUGUSTA.

I am not used to rise till eight. How shall I ever contrive to be ready?

HENRY.

I will rouse you, by ringing of the bell.

Mrs. HARCOURT.

Late rising is a bad habit, that you have been allowed to contract; but my dear Augusta, determine to overcome it; it will require a little resolution at first, but when you consider the advantages it will procure, I am persuaded the difficulty will appear trifling. Health and opportunity for improvement, result from an early hour; a pale face, languor, and slothfulness, are the penalties of lying long in bed. A too great proportion of sleep is equally a species of intemperance with gluttony and drunkenness, and yet many persons, who would shudder at being accused of those depravities, freely indulge themselves in the former, from want of consideration, ill example, and long habit; and by that means injure their constitutions, and lose a large portion of the active part of their lives. Perhaps the building of this grotto may be the fortunate means of accustoming you to wake at a proper hour, and when you once have used yourself to it, you will find it both pleasant and profitable.

AUGUSTA.

You have convinced me of the advantage of rising early, and I shall endeavour to be one of the first at the grove. Papa has lately given me a fine pearl necklace that was mamma's: my governess tells me that they are not beads, but that they are found in oysters. I thought I would enquire the next time we met, how they came there, as I suppose they are no part of the fish.

Mr. HARCOURT.

Many have been the conjectures of both ancient and modern writers concerning the production of pearls. Some have supposed them to proceed from a disease of the fish; but there seems to be a great similarity between them, and what is found in crabs, called crabs-eyes, which are formed near the stomach of the animal, and serve as a reservoir of calcareous matter against the forming of a new shell, at which time they are dissolved, and deposited for that purpose. As the internal part of the shell of the pearl, oyster, or muscle, consists of mother pearl, which resembles the material of pearl, and as the animal has annually occasion to enlarge his shell, there is reason to suspect that the loose pearls are similar reservoirs of the pearly matter for that purpose. The fish, in which the pearls are found, is much larger than the common oyster, and is called concha margaritifera. It abounds on the coast of Persia, near Ormus, about Cape Comorin, and on the coast of the island of Ceylon. The oriental pearls are most valued on account of their largeness, colour, and beauty; but pearls are caught in the seas of the East-Indies, in those of America, and in some parts of Europe. At the commencement of the season, which is in March and April, and again in August and September, there appear frequently two hundred and fifty barks on the banks; in the larger are two divers; in the smaller, one. Each bark puts off from shore before sun-rise, by a land-breeze which never fails, and returns again by a sea-breeze, which succeeds it at noon. As soon as the barks have arrived at the place where the fish lie, and have cast anchor, each diver binds a stone under his body, which is to serve him as ballast, and prevent his being driven away by the motion of the water, and also to enable him to walk more steadily among the waves. Besides

61

this, they tie another heavy stone to one foot, in order to sink them to the bottom of the sea: and as the oysters adhere strongly to the rocks, they arm their fingers with leather gloves, or take an iron-rake to displace them with. Lastly, each diver carries with him a large net, tied to his neck by a long cord, the other end which is fastened to the side of the bark. The net or sack is intended to hold the oysters he may collect, and the cord is to pull him up by, when his bag is full, or when he wants air. Thus equipped, he precipitates himself, sometimes above sixty feet under water. As he has no time to lose, as soon as he arrives at the bottom, he begins to tear the oysters off the rocks and cram them into his budget. At what ever depth the divers are, the light is sufficient for them to see what-passes around them, and sometimes, to their great consternation, they behold monstrous fishes from whose jaws they can escape only by mudding the water, and concealing themselves by that means; although this artifice will not always save them from falling a prey to these formidable enemies. The best divers will remain under water near half an hour, during which time they hold their breath, without the use of oils, acquiring the habit by long practice; but the exertion is so violent, as generally to shorten the lives of those who repeat it frequently. Besides this method of diving, there is a way of descending in a diving bell, so contrived as to be replenished often with fresh air, by means of air-barrels, which are let up and down by ropes.

SOPHIA.

The dangers that the poor diver incurs, to obtain a mere bauble, for I suppose pearls are only used for ornaments, are far more dreadful than those of the Greenland fisherman.

Mrs. HARCOURT.

The poor men, who encounter these dangers for a livelihood, do not consider how trifling the value of the pearls is in itself, but what great advantages they can gain by the risk. Single pearls have been sold for immense sums of money. Cleopatra, queen of Egypt, wore one as an earring, that Pliny has estimated at eighty-thousand pounds sterling. The real value of pearls and diamonds is small, because they do not contribute to the support or comfort of the life of man; but whilst people of fortune will lavish great sums upon such insignificant things, there will always be found people, whose necessities will impel them to obtain them at the risk of these lives.

It is time to separate. Remember, our appointment in the grove at six tomorrow morning.

CONVERSATION 9

Mr. HARCOURT.

WELL, ladies, how have you proceeded with your grotto? Though I am not one of the party, I am interested in your success.

SOPHIA.

We go on very well indeed, Charles has drawn the plan, and mamma has given James leave to help my brother to dig the foundations; Augusta and Cecilia are employed in sorting and cleaning the shells and fossils; they also have undertaken to collect pebbles, and gather mosses, attended by little Henry, who carries a basket to put them in; and I am very busy making artificial coral; thus we all take a share. Mamma is so kind as to promise us a present of shells and ores; and, if you please, you must contribute, by procuring us some glass cinders, or refuse of the furnaces from the glass-house.

Mr. HARCOURT.

Most willingly shall I supply you with that, or any other thing you may want, to forward your design; but pray, can any of you inform me, of what ingredients glass is composed?

CHARLES.

I think, Sir, you have told me that the principal articles in its composition are salt and sand, or some kind of stone which answers the same purpose; the salt must be of the fixed kind, such as will not evaporate with the most intense heat, and is generally procured from the ashes of a vegetable called kali, which is brought from the Levant. The sand or stone, must be such as will melt easily, which gives firmness and consistence to the glass.

Mr. HARCOURT.

The best stone for this purpose, comes also from Italy, and is called tarso. But sand is now almost the only substance employed in the British manufactures of glass. The most suitable is that which is white, small, and shining; when examined by the microscope, it appears to be fragments of rock crystal; that which is of a soft texture, and more gritty, does very well for green glass. Our

64

glass-houses are furnished with white sand for their crystal glasses, from Lynn in Norfolk, and Maidstone in Kent; and with the coarser, for green glass, from Woolwich; other ingredients are occasionally mixed with these, according to the kind of glass required, such as arsenic, manganese, lead, &c.

Mrs. HARCOURT.

Sophia, you have seen a glass-house, cannot you give some account of the operations performed there?

SOPHIA.

There are three sorts of furnaces used in the glass-works. After having properly mixed the ashes and sand together, they are put into the first furnace, where they are burned or calcined for a sufficient time, and become what is called frit, which being boiled in pots or crucibles of pipe-maker's clay, in the second furnace, is rendered fit for blowing.

AUGUSTA.

How very extraordinary that materials of so gross and dirty a nature, should ever become so beautiful and transparent as glass! By what is the alteration occasioned?

Mrs. HARCOURT.

The metamorphosis, for it may well be termed so, is caused by the action of the fire, which when intense, vitrifies or turns them into glass. Sophia, go on with your account.

SOPHIA.

The workman, who blows the glass, takes his blowing iron, which is a hollow tube about two feet and a half long, and dipping it in the melting-pot, turns it about: the metal sticks to the iron like honey: he dips four times for every glass, and at every dip, rolls the end of his instrument, with the glass on it, on a piece of iron, over which is a vessel of water, which by its coolness consolidates the glass, and disposes it to bind better with the next to be taken out of the pot. When he has got enough of matter on the instrument, he begins to blow gently through it, in the same manner as boys blow soap-suds through a pipe, and in order to give it a polish, he rolls it backwards and forwards on a stone or marble: after blowing, and whirling the iron till he has formed the glass to the intended shape, he delivers it to the master workman to break off the collet, which is a little piece that sticks to the iron. In order to hollow it out, another workman thrusts in an iron instrument, and turns it round with a circular motion till it is sufficiently enlarged. When it is perfectly formed, it is set in the lear or third furnace, to anneal or harden; it is proper to add, that the stem, and the foot of a drinking glass, require each a distinct operation.

Mrs. HARCOURT.

Habit and long practice enable these men to endure these scorching heats, which they receive directly in their faces, mouths and lungs. They are always obliged to work in their shirts, with a broad brimmed straw hat on their heads, to preserve their eyes from the excessive heat and light. They sit in large wide wooden chairs, with long elbows, to which their instruments are hung. They work for six hours without intermission, when they are relieved by another set of workmen, who take their places for the same space of time.

CECILIA.

Panes of glass for windows cannot surely be formed by blowing, pray how are they made?

Mr. HARCOURT.

The workman contrives to blow and dispose his glass so as to form a cylinder, which by frequently heating and working on a kind of earthen table, at length begins to open and unfold like a sheet of paper, a previous notch or incision being made for that purpose in the cylinder of glass, and thus it becomes flat; the table of glass is now nearly perfected, and requires nothing farther but to be heated over again. When taken out, they lay it on a table of copper from whence it is carried to the third furnace to anneal.

HENRY.

Pray explain the meaning of that word, I do not understand it.

Mr. HARCOURT.

It signifies to bake or harden; the first furnace in a glass-house is heated to an intense degree of heat, in order to fuse or incorporate the ingredients; the second is also heated sufficiently to melt and vitrify the frit into a glassy substance; but the third is moderately heated, that it may perform the office of baking or hardening the work, when fashioned to the shape it is to bear.

HENRY.

You have explained this so clearly, that I am no longer at a loss to comprehend it.

Mr. HARCOURT.

There are two methods of making plates for looking-glasses; the one, by blowing them much in the same manner as they blow glass for windows, but on a larger scale. The other, casting or running of them, which is generally practised in making large glasses. The French claim the honour of this invention. It was first proposed to the French court in 1688, by the Sieur Abraham Thevart. It is performed in nearly a similar manner to the casting of sheet-lead, and this method not only enables them to make glasses of more than double the size of any made by blowing but also to cast all kinds of borders, mouldings, &c. The furnaces for melting the materials of this manufacture are of enormous size and those for annealing the glasses, when formed, still larger. There are at least twenty-four annealing furnaces or ovens, each above twenty feet long, placed around a melting furnace. All these furnaces are covered over with a large shed, under which are likewise built forges and workhouses for smiths, carpenters, and other artificers who are continually employed in repairing and keeping in order the machines, furnaces, &c. as also apartments for these, and the workmen employed about the glass. So that the glass-house in the castle of St. Gobin, in the forest of Fere, in the Soissonois, celebrated for its excellence in this manufacture, appears more like a little city, than an assemblage of workmen's sheds. The insides of the furnaces are lined with a sort of baked earth, adapted to sustain the action of fire, and the same earth serves also for melting-pots, cisterns, &c. The cisterns are about a yard long, and half as wide, they serve for the conveyance of liquid glass, which is drawn out of the melting-pots, to the casting tables. When the matter is sufficiently vitrified, refined, and settled, they fill the cisterns, and leave them in the furnace, till they appear white through excessive heat. The table on which the glass is to be run, is of cast-iron. There is a curious machinery to remove the cisterns from the furnaces to the table, which places them in an inclined position, so as to discharge a torrent of matter, like liquid fire, with which the table is presently covered. As soon as the glass is come to a consistence, they shove it off into the annealing furnace, with an iron raker as wide as the table, being assisted by workmen on the other side of the furnace, who pull it to them with iron hooks.

CHARLES.

I cannot imagine how they contrive to remove them in that burning state, without either breaking the glasses, or hurting themselves.

Mr. HARCOURT.

The surprising dexterity and quickness with which they perform the different operations, is inconceivable to those who have not been eye-witnesses of that wonderful manufacture. The tisors, or persons employed in heating the large furnaces, run round the furnace in their shirts, without the least intermission, with a speed scarce inferior to that of the lightest courier: as they go along, they take two billets of wood, and throw them into the first furnace, and continuing their course, do the same for the second. This they hold on uninterruptedly for six hours together. One would not expect, that two such small pieces of wood, which are consumed in an instant, would maintain the furnace in the proper degree of heat, which is so great, that a large bar of iron, laid at one of the mouths of the furnace, becomes red hot in less than half a minute. The process of these glasses is now completed, except grinding, polishing, and foliating, or laying on of the quicksilver. The grinding of glass requires great nicety, when performed on glasses that are designed for telescopes, or other optical uses. Plate or cast glass is ground by placing it on a stone table, in such a manner, that it cannot be shaken or displaced, and then by means of a wooden frame, another glass is rubbed backwards and forwards over it with water and sand between them, and thus by constant attrition their surfaces become smooth.

Mrs. HARCOURT.

Various are the uses to which the ingenious invention of glass is applied; besides the different accommodations with which it supplies domestic wants, such as windows, looking-glasses, and all the innumerable variety of vessels that adorn our tables, and contribute to our convenience. Natural philosophy is greatly assisted by telescopes, microscopes, magnifying glasses, &c. which enable us to view objects too minute, or too distant ever to be examined by the naked eye. Many experiments in electricity, and on the properties of the air, the knowledge of which is called pneumatics, could not be performed without the assistance of glass. The eye-sight of aged persons, or those who have a defective sight, receive relief from spectacles, which they must have sought in vain, without this invention. They were the fortunate discovery of a monk of Pisa, in the year 1299. Nor does it only serve for useful purposes: it also supplies us with various kinds of ornaments. Most of the precious stones are so well imitated by this composition, as to deceive the eye of those who are not critical judges.

CHARLES.

Among the variety you have enumerated, you have omitted burning glasses, which are so contrived, that they draw the sun's rays into one point or focus, and are capable of setting fire to any thing that will burn. Some historians relate, that Archimedes, the celebrated mathematician of Syracuse, invented glasses of this kind, so powerful, that they set fire to the Roman ships, besieging Syracuse, under the command of Marcellus, and destroyed the whole fleet. Thus the ingenuity and invention of one man was able to resist and repel the united force of thousands, under the command of the most accomplished general of his age and country.

Mr. HARCOURT.

Your historical anecdote is very suitably introduced, and is an eminent instance of the superiority of wisdom over brutal strength.

SOPHIA.

Has not the invention of the armonica some claim to be mentioned, before we dismiss this subject?

Mrs. HARCOURT.

I am not surprised it should be recollected by a lover of music; but Sophia, you must not raise curiosity without satisfying it; perhaps some of the company may not know what an armonica is.

SOPHIA.

The armonica is a musical instrument, peculiar for the sweetness of its tones, and consists of glasses, of the shape of a globe, cut in half. The whole set is fixed upon a spindle, and then played upon by turning them round with a wet finger.

Mr. HARCOURT.

This method of producing musical sounds, though first introduced among us by Mr. Puckeridge of Ireland, has been long since practised in Germany: and the Persians have also a similar invention, by striking seven cups of porcelain, containing a certain quantity of water, with small sticks.

CECILIA.

Among the other curiosities made of glass, give me leave to mention Rupert's drops, which are formed somewhat in the shape of a pear, of green glass, and though they will bear the heaviest stroke of a hammer without breaking, fly to pieces in a moment, if you break off the tip of the tail.

HENRY.

Pray, of what did they make windows before there was any glass? I can think of nothing that would keep out the cold, and be clear at the same time.

Mrs. HARCOURT.

Horn and oiled paper were the substitutes they were obliged to use. Glass windows were not known in England till 1180; and then were considered as a mark of great magnificence, suitable only to palaces, churches, &c. The Italians possessed this art first. The French learned it of them, and from thence it was brought into England. Venice for many years excelled all Europe in the fineness of its glasses: and in the thirteenth century, were the only people that had the secret of making crystal looking-glasses. The glass manufacture was first begun in England in 1557. Glass plates were made at Lambeth, in 1673, under the patronage of the Duke of Buckingham, who introduced this manufacture into England, with amazing success. So that in a century we have attained the art in a degree, that rivals even the Venetians, and are no longer obliged to be supplied with this article from foreign countries.

AUGUSTA.

What beautiful painted windows I have sometimes observed in churches. There is one in Norwich cathedral, that is reckoned to be very finely painted, done by Mrs. Lloyd, who was the wife of one of the deans. Papa was acquainted with her, and he says she added many other elegant accomplishments to her skill in painting on glass.

Mrs. HARCOURT.

Remark how much better this lady's leisure was employd, than it would have been in idle dissipation, or slothful indolence; her works remain a testimony of her industry and taste, and will long preserve her name from oblivion. The ancient manner of painting on glass was very simple, and consisted in the mere arrangement of pieces of glass of different colours, in some sort of symmetry, and constituted a species of what we call mosaic work. In time, the taste for this kind of work improved, and the art being found applicable to the adorning of churches and other public buildings, they found means of incorporating the colours with the glass itself, by exposing them to a proper degree of fire, after the colours are laid on.

Mr. HARCOURT.

There is an easy method of painting small pictures on glass, called back-painting, which requires but little skill, and produces a pretty effect. You must take a piece of crown glass, the size of the print you intend to paint, a metzotinto is the best adapted to the purpose; soak your print in clean water for forty-eight hours, if it be on very strong, close, hard gummed paper; but if on a soft spongy paper, two hours will be sufficient; then lay the print between four sheets of paper, two beneath it, and two above it, that the moisture may be drawn out of it. In the meanwhile, let the glass be warmed at the fire, then with a hogs-hair brush dipped in melted Strasburg turpentine, smear the glass smoothly and evenly. Lay the print upon the glass, rubbing it gently from one end to the other, that it may lie close. With the finger rub off the paper from the backside of the print, till nothing can be seen, but the print, like a thin film upon the glass, and set it aside to dry. When it is well dried, varnish it over with some white transparent varnish, that the print may be seen through it, which is now fit for painting. Having prepared a variety of oil colours, which must be ground very fine, and tempered very stiff, lay such colours on the transparent print as your fancy and taste direct; the outlines of the print guiding the pencil, and it will produce a very pretty effect. You must be careful to lay on the colours thick enough to appear plainly through the glass. When your grotto is finished, you may exercise yourselves this way, and each one produce a picture, though much inferior to those works that require the hand of an artist, yet affording amusement for a leisure hour, and varying the course of your occupations. Adieu my dear children; I wish you repose and pleasant dreams.

CONVERSATION 10

HENRY.

MAY I be allowed to chuse a subject for this evening. I want to know what sugar is made of. I heard Mr. Jenkins say it was a salt, and I think he must be mistaken, for I cannot taste the least flavour of salt in it.

Mr. HARCOURT.

Chemically considered, he is in the right. Sugar is a sweet, agreeable, saline juice, expressed from many different kinds of vegetables. Carrots, parsnips, white and red beets yield sugar, but the plant, from which the sugar, that is generally used, is procured, is the sugar-cane; a sort of reed that grows in great plenty, in both the East and West-Indies. Sophia, endeavour to give us a botanical definition of it.

SOPHIA.

It is a genus of the triandria digynia class. Its characters are, that it has no empalement; but instead of it, a woolly down longer than the flower that incloses it. The flower is bivalve, the valves are oblong, acute pointed, concave, and chaffy. It has three hairs like stamina, the ends of the valves terminated by oblong summits; and an awl-shaped germen, supporting two rough styles, crowned by single stigmas, the germen becomes an oblong, acute pointed seed, invested by the valves. It is cultivated in both the Indies for its juice, which when boiled, affords that sweet salt which is called sugar.

Mr. HARCOURT.

The canes grow from eight to twenty feet high, they are jointed, and at each joint are placed leaves. They are propagated by cuttings, which are generally taken from the tops of the canes, just below the leaves; a deep soil and light land are most suitable to the sugar-plant, and the rainy season is the proper time for planting it. The ground should be marked out by a line, that the canes may be regularly disposed, and at equal distances. The common method of planting them, is to make a trench with a hoe, which is performed by the hand; into this trench a negro drops the number of cuttings intended to be planted, which are planted by other negroes, who follow him: and the earth is drawn about the hills with a hoe.

CHARLES.

I fancy agriculture is not so well understood in the Indies, as it is in Europe: or they would make use of the plough in these operations; as it would perform the work both more expeditiously, and in a completer manner, than can be done by the hand. What length of time and what multitudes of hands, would it occupy, to hoe up all the land in England, that is to be sowed with corn every season!

Mr. HARCOURT.

Horses are very scarce in the West-Indies especially, and almost all laborious operations are performed by the hands of negro slaves.

AUGUSTA.

Are those countries inhabited by negroes? I understood that they were the natives of Africa.

Mr. HARCOURT.

You were rightly informed, my dear, they are indeed natives of Africa, but snatched from their own country, friends, and connections, by the hand of violence, and power. I am ashamed to confess that many ships are annually sent from different parts of England, particularly Bristol and Liverpool, to the coast of Guinea, to procure slaves from that unhappy country, for the use of our West-India islands, where they are sold to the planters of sugar-plantations, in an open market like cattle, and afterwards employed in the most laborious and servile occupations, and pass the rest of their lives in an involuntary and wretched slavery.

SOPHIA.

How much my heart feels for them! How terrible must it be to be separated from one's near relations! Parents perhaps divided from their children for ever; husbands from their wives; brothers and sisters obliged to take an eternal farewel. Why do the kings of the African states suffer their subjects to be so cruelly treated?

Mrs. HARCOURT.

Many causes have operated to induce the African princes to become assistants in this infamous traffic, and instead of being the

74

defenders of their harmless people, they have frequently betrayed them to their cruellest enemies. The Europeans have found the means of corrupting these ignorant rulers, with bribes of rum and other spirituous liquors, of which they are immoderately fond. At other times they have fomented jealousies, and excited wars between them, merely for the sake of obtaining the prisoners of war for slaves. Frequently they use no ceremony, but go on shore in the night, set fire to a neighbouring village and seize upon all the unhappy victims, who run out to escape the flames.

CECILIA.

What hardened hearts must the captains of those ships have! They must have become extremely cruel before they would undertake such an employment.

Mrs. HARCOURT.

It is much to be feared that most of them, by the habits of such a life, are become deaf to the voice of pity; but we must compassionate the situation of those, whose parents have early bred them to this profession, before they were of an age to chuse a different employment. But to resume the subject of the negroes. What I have related is only the beginning of their sorrows. When they are put on board the ships, they are crowded together in the hold, where many of them mostly die from want of air and room. There have been frequent instances of their throwing themselves into the sea, when they could find an opportunity, and seeking a refuge from their misfortunes in death. As soon as they arrive in the West-Indies, they are carried to a public market, where they are sold to the best bidder, like horses at our fairs. Their future lot depends much upon the disposition of the master, into whose hands they happen to fall, for among the overseers of sugar-plantations there are some men of feeling and humanity; but too generally their treatment is very severe. Accustomed to an inactive indolent life, in the luxurious and plentiful country of Africa, they find great hardship from the transition, to a life of severe labour, without any mixture of indulgence to soften it. Deprived of hope of amending their condition, by any course of conduct they can pursue, they frequently abandon themselves to despair, and die, in what is called the seasoning, which is becoming inured by length of time to their situation. Those who have less sensibility and stronger constitutions, survive their complicated misery but a few years: for it is generally acknowledged that they seldom attain the full period of human life.

AUGUSTA.

Humanity shudders at your account; but I have heard a gentleman, that had lived many years abroad, say, that negroes were not much superior to the brutes, and that they were so stupid and stubborn, that nothing but stripes and severity could have any influence over them.

Mr. HARCOURT.

That gentleman was most probably interested in misleading those with whom he conversed. People, who argue in that manner, do not consider the disadvantages the poor negroes suffer from want of cultivation. Leading an ignorant savage life in their own country, they can have acquired no previous information: and when they fall into the hands of their cruel oppressors, a life of laborious servitude, which scarcely affords them sufficient time for sleep, deprives them of every opportunity of improving their minds. There is no reason to suppose that they differ from us in anything but colour, which distinction arises from the intense heat of their climate. There have been instances of a few, whose situation has been favourable to improvement, that have shewn no inferiority of capacity: and those masters, who neglect the religious and moral instruction of their slaves, add a heavy load of guilt to that already incurred, by their share in this unjust and inhuman traffic.

CHARLES.

My indignation arises at this recital. Why does not the British parliament exert its power, to avenge the wrongs of these oppressed Africans? What can prevent an act being passed to forbid Englishmen from buying and selling slaves?

Mr. HARCOURT.

Mr. Wilberforce,* a name that does honour to humanity, has

---

* William Wilberforce (1759-1833), M.P. and the leading social welfare activist of

made several fruitless efforts to obtain an act for the abolition of this trade. Men, interested in its continuance, have hitherto frustrated his noble design; but we may rely upon the goodness of that Divine Providence, that careth for all creatures, that the day will come, that their rights will be considered and there is great reason to hope, from the light already cast upon the subject, that the rising generation will prefer justice and mercy, to interest and policy: and will free themselves from the odium we at present suffer, of treating our fellow-creatures in a manner unworthy of them, and of ourselves.

Mrs. HARCOURT.

Henry, repeat that beautiful apostrophe to a negro woman, which you learned the other day out of Mrs. Barbauld's Hymns.*

HENRY.

"Negro woman, who sittest pining in captivity, and weepest over thy sick child, though no one seeth thee, God seeth thee, though no one pitieth thee, God pitieth thee. Raise thy voice, forlorn, and abandoned one; call upon him from amidst thy bonds, for assuredly he will hear thee."

CECILIA.

I think no riches could tempt me to have any share in the slave-trade. I could never enjoy peace of mind, whilst I thought I contributed to the woes of my fellow-creatures.

Mr. HARCOURT.

But Cecilia, to put your compassion to the proof; are you willing to debar yourself of the many indulgencies that we enjoy, that are

---

his day, became parliamentary leader in 1788 of the campaign for the abolition of slavery. The motion for gradual abolition carried in 1791, but the full bill did not receive royal assent until 1807.

* Anna Laetitia Barbauld's widely-reprinted *Hymns in Prose for Children* (1781) were "intended to be committed to memory and recited" as a way "to impress devotional figures as early as possible on the infant mind" (Preface).

the fruit of their labour? sugar, coffee, rice, calico, rum, and many other things, are procured by the sweat of their brow.

CECILIA.

I would forego any indulgence to alleviate their sufferings.

The rest of the Children together.

We are all of the same mind.

Mrs. HARCOURT.

I admire the sensibility of your uncorrupted hearts, my dear children. It is the voice of nature and virtue. Listen to it on all occasions, and bring it home to your bosoms, and your daily practice. The same principle of benevolence, which excites your just indignation at the oppression of the negroes, will lead you to be gentle towards your inferiors, kind and obliging to your equals, and in a particular manner condescending and considerate towards your domestics; requiring no more of them, than you would be willing to perform in their situation; instructing them when you have opportunity; sympathizing in their afflictions, and promoting their best interests when in your power.

AUGUSTA.

My governess forbids me ever to speak to the servants, therefore I cannot shew them any kindness, without disobeying her.

Mrs. HARCOURT.

Your governess shews her discretion in forbidding you to be familiar with the servants. Their want of education renders them improper companions, but can never deprive them of their claim to our tenderness and good offices.

Mr. HARCOURT.

It is time to proceed in our account of the process of preparing the juice of the sugar-cane for use. When the canes are ripe, they are cut, and carried in bundles to the mill. The mills consist of three wooden rollers, covered with steel-plates, and are set in motion, either by water, wind, cattle, or even the hands of slaves. The juice being squeezed out of the canes, by the rollers, runs through a little canal into the sugar-house, where it falls into a vessel, from whence it is conveyed into the first copper. With the liquor is mixed a quantity of ashes and quick-lime, which serves to purify it, by raising up the unctuous matter in form of a scum to the top, which is skimmed off and given to poultry. This operation is performed five or six times, till the sugar is sufficiently purified, and become of a proper thickness to be converted into the various kinds for use. It is then put into hogsheads, and sent over to England to the care of the sugar-refiners, whose business it is to complete the process, by boiling it up with bullock's blood in order to clear it. Sometimes whites of eggs are used for the same purpose. They add a little of the finest indigo to give it a good colour. It is boiled over again, that the moist parts may evaporate. The next thing to be done is to fill the moulds, which are in the form of inverted cones. The rooms in which these moulds are placed, are heated to a suitable degree, to dry the sugar they contain. When the loaves are fully dried, they are papered, and sold to the grocer.

HENRY.

Are sugar-candy and barley-sugar made from the sugar-cane? They are different from sugar both in taste and colour.

Mr. HARCOURT.

The material is the same, although the preparation varies. Sugar-candy is sugar crystallized. It is first dissolved in a weak lime-water, then clarified, scummed, strained through a cloth, and boiled. It is afterwards put into forms or moulds, that are crossed with threads to retain the sugar as it crystallizes. These forms are suspended in a hot stove, which is shut up, and the fire made very vehement. Upon this, the sugar fastens to the strings that cross the forms, and there hangs in little splinters of crystal. When the sugar is quite dry, the forms are broken, and the sugar is taken out candied. Red sugar-candy is coloured, by pouring a little juice of the Indian fig into the vessel, whilst the sugar is boiling. Barley-sugar, is sugar boiled till it is brittle, and then poured on a stone anointed with oil of sweet almonds, and formed into twisted sticks. It should be boiled up with a decoction of barley, whence it takes its name; they sometimes cast saffron into it, to give it the bright amber colour.

Mrs. HARCOURT.

Sugar is a very useful commodity. It preserves both animal and vegetable substances from putrefaction; and we are indebted to it, on this account, for all the variety of conserves and sweetmeats which adorn and enrich our repasts. White sugar candy is used by miniature painters to prevent the colours from cracking, when mixed with gum arabic; and Henry need not be told how useful barley-sugar is in coughs and hoarsenesses.

Mr. HARCOURT.

It is supposed that, although the ancients were acquainted with this plant, they were ignorant of our method of refining and preparing it. The first account we have of sugar-refiners in England, is in the year 1659. Several other things are produced from the sugar-cane. Treacle is the syrup that runs from the barrels of raw sugar. Rum is distilled from the sugar-cane.

CHARLES.

Is not arrack also made from sugar?

Mr. HARCOURT.

It is sometimes distilled from rice and sugar, fermented with the juice of cocoanuts; but it is generally distilled from a vegetable juice called toddy, which flows, by incision, out of the cocoa-nut tree, like the birch juice procured among us for wine. The sugar-house of a refiner is a large building, consisting of six or seven floors, and the utensils necessary to perform the different operation, require the aid of various kinds of workmen. The pans, coolers, cisterns, syrup-pipes, basons, ladles, skimmers, and sometimes the candy-pots are made of copper. Pipes, pumps, and cisterns made of lead are also used. The iron founder supplies bars of a triangular form to be laid under the pans; also the cockel, which is an iron trunk used to dry the goods in the stove, iron doors &c. The carpenter is required to furnish racks, troughs, stools, blocks, coolers, oars, &c. Tubs and backs to hold the lime-water which contain from thirty to two hundred barrels, employ the back-maker. The wicker-work consists of refining-baskets, scum-baskets, pulling-up baskets, coal and clay-baskets, &c. Thus, if we consider the numbers employed in building the ships used in bringing over the sugar, and in conveying the poor slaves from their own country; planters, overseers, &c. we may suppose that we do not taste a lump of sugar that is not produced by the united labour of a thousand hands.

SOPHIA.

And yet we use the conveniencies of life in a careless wasteful manner, without reflecting one moment on the trouble necessary to procure them. May I relate the manner of obtaining the maple-sugar, which some have endeavoured to introduce in the room of the produce of the sugar-cane.

Mrs. HARCOURT.

By all means; it will give us pleasure to hear it.

SOPHIA.

The acer saccharinum, or the sugar-maple-tree, grows in great quantities in the western countries of all the middle states of the American Union. These trees are generally found mixed with the beech, hemlock, white and water-ash, the cucumber-tree, linden, aspen, butter-nut, and wild cherry-trees. They grow only on the richest soils, and frequently in stony ground. Springs of the purest water abound in their neighbourhood. They are, when fully grown, as tall as the white and black oaks, and from two to three feet in diameter. They put forth a beautiful white blossom in the spring before they shew a single leaf. The wood of the maple tree is extremely inflammable. Its small branches are so much impregnated with sugar, as to afford support to the cattle, horses, and sheep of the first settlers, during the winter, before they are able to cultivate forage for that purpose. Its ashes afford a great quantity of pot-ash exceeded by a few of the trees that grow in the woods of the United States. The tree is supposed to arrive at its full growth in twenty years. It is not injured by tapping; on the contrary, the oftener it is tapped, the more syrup it yields. The effects of a yearly discharge of sap from the tree, in improving and increasing the sap, are demonstrated from the superior excellence of those trees, which have been perforated in an hundred places, by a small wood-pecker, which feeds upon the sap. The method of obtaining the sap, is by boring a hole in the tree, with an auger; a spout is introduced about half an inch into the hole, made by the auger. The sap flows from four to six weeks, according to the temperature of the weather. Troughs are placed under the spout to receive the sap, which is carried every day to a large receiver, whence it is conveyed, after being strained, to the boiler. There are three modes of reducing the sap to sugar; by evaporation, by freezing, and by boiling, of which the latter is most expeditious. The profit of this tree is not confined to its sugar. It affords a most agreeable molasses, and an excellent vinegar. The sap, which is suitable for these purposes, is obtained, after the sap which affords the sugar has ceased to flow, so that the manufactories of these different products of the maple-tree, by succeeding, do not interfere with each other. The molasses may be used to compose the basis of a pleasant summer beer. The sap of the maple is moreover capable of affording a spirit. A tree so various in its uses, if duly cultivated, may one day supply us with sugar; and silence the arguments of the planters, for a continuance of the slave trade.

Mr. HARCOURT.

Very philosophically observed. We thank you for your entertaining account and wish you good-night, as it is already past the usual time of separation.

CONVERSATION 11

CECILIA.

I THANK you, dear mamma, in the name of my brothers and sister, for the pleasure you have given us, in allowing us to accept Farmer Dobson's invitation to his sheep-shearing. We have passed a very agreeable afternoon, both from the civility of the honest farmer and his wife, and the novelty of the scene, which was very striking to us, as we had never seen any thing of the kind before. It reminded me of Thomson's* description of a sheep-shearing, which with your leave I will repeat.

Mrs. HARCOURT.

It will give me pleasure to hear it, provided you are careful to speak slow, distinct, and give every word its proper emphasis.

CECILIA.

> "In one diffusive band,
> They drive the troubled flocks, by many a dog
> Compell'd, to where the mazy running brook
> Forms a deep pool; this bank abrupt and high,
> And that fair-spreading in a pebbled shore,
> Urg'd to the giddy brink, much is the toil,
> The clamour much, of men, and boys, and dogs,
> Ere the soft fearful people to the flood
> Commit their woolly sides. And oft the swain,
> On some impatient seizing, hurls them in:
> Emboldened then, nor hesitating more,
> Fast, fast, they plunge amid the flashing wave,
> And, panting, labour to the farthest shore.
> Repeated this, till deep the well-wash'd fleece
> Has drunk the flood, and from his lively haunt
> The trout is banish'd by the sordid stream;
> Heavy, and dripping, to the breezy brow
> Slow move the harmless race: where, as they spread
> Their swelling treasures to the sunny ray,

---

* James Thomson's *The Seasons* (1746), "Summer": 371-422.

Inly disturb'd, and wondering what this wild
Outrageous tumult means, their loud complaints
The country fill; and, toss'd from rock to rock,
Incessant bleatings run around the hills.
At last, of snowy white, the gathered flocks
Are in the wattled pen innumerous press'd,
Head above head; and rang'd in lusty rows,
The shepherds sit, and whet the sounding shears.
The housewife waits to roll her fleecy stores,
With all her gay-dressed maids attending round.
One, chief, in gracious dignity enthron'd,
Shines o'er the rest, the pastoral queen, and rays
Her smiles, sweet beaming, on her shepherd king;
While the glad circle round them yield their souls
To festive mirth, and wit that knows no gall.
Meantime, their joyous talk goes on apace:
Some mingling stir the melted tar; and some,
Deep on the new-shorn vagrant's heaving side
To stamp his mother's cypher ready stand;
Others th' unwilling wedder drag along;
And, glorying in his might, the sturdy boy
Holds by the twisted horns th' indignant ram.
Behold, where bound, and of its robe bereft,
By needy man, that all-depending lord,
How meek, how patient, the mild creature lies!
What softness in its melancholy face,
What dumb complaining innocence appears!
Fear not, ye gentle tribes, 'tis not the knife
Of horrid slaughter, that is o'er you wav'd,
No, 'tis the tender swain's well-guided shears,
Who having now, to pay his annual care,
Borrow'd your fleece, to you a cumbrous load,
Will send you bounding to your hills again.

Mrs. HARCOURT.

Tolerably well repeated; a general acquaintance with the best
English poets, united with a retentive memory and graceful enun-
ciation, will furnish the rare and delightful accomplishment of
repeating selected passages, which may supply an elegant amusement for the vacant hour of domestic leisure, and prevent that
lassitude so frequently complained of at home, and which compels

so many to seek a refuge from themselves in dissipation and fashionable pleasure.

SOPHIA.

My time is so variously filled up, that I never experience that wearisomeness.

Mrs. HARCOURT.

A well chosen succession of employments, is the best antidote against *ennui,* as it is termed by the French, or listlessness. Reading, drawing, natural history in its different branches, simple mathematics, experimental philosophy, with various other rational pursuits, are admirably calculated to fill up the leisure hours of persons in easy circumstances, whose duties or business afford them opportunity for such studies.

Mr. HARCOURT.

It is a just observation, that none but the idle want employment. The active mind collects amusement from the most trifling events. Cannot a sheep-shearing supply us with a hint for the subject of our present conversation? Sophia, endeavour to entertain us with the natural history of the sheep.

SOPHIA.

Sheep, according to Linnaeus, are of the order of pecora, and make a distinct genus, the characters which distinguish them, are that their horns are hollow, bent backward, wreathed, crooked, and scabrous. They have eight cutting teeth in the lower jaw, but none in the upper, and no canine teeth. The wool of these animals consists only of long slender hairs, much twisted, and variously interwoven with one another. This cloathing is peculiar to the sheep kind, so far as is yet known, no other animal having been discovered with a similar covering; neither is it possessed by all the species of sheep, some of those of the distant nations have short hair like that of the goat.

Mr. HARCOURT.

In addition to your general account of the sheep, I will enumerate the species, and their peculiarities, which according to the same great master of natural arrangement, Linnaeus, are three; first the ovis aris, or ram sheep, which comprehends many varieties, such as the common sheep, with large horns twisting spirally and outwardly: the hornless sheep, with the tail hanging down to the knees; this kind is common in many parts of England. The Spanish, or many horned sheep, having usually three horns, and sometimes four or five. This sort of sheep is frequent in Iceland, Siberia, and other northern countries. The African sheep, which has short hair like that of the goat; and the broad-tailed sheep, which is common in Syria, Barbary, and Ethiopia. The tails of these are so long, as to trail upon the ground, and the shepherds are obliged to put boards with small wheels under them, to keep them from galling. These tails are esteemed a great delicacy, being of a substance between fat and marrow; they sometimes weigh fifty pounds each. The broad-tailed sheep are also found in the kingdom of Thibet, and their fleeces are equal to those of Caramania in fineness, beauty, and length. The Cackemirians engross this article, and have factors in all parts of Thibet, for buying up the wool, which they work up into those elegant shawls, that are brought into this country from the East-Indies, and this manufacture supplies them with a considerable source of wealth. The second species is the ovis Guiniensis, commonly called the Angola sheep, They are long-legged and tall, and their ears hang down, the horns are small and bending down to the eyes. The neck is adorned with a long mane, the hair of the rest of the body is short, and it has wattles on the neck. The third species is the ovis strepsiciros, or Cretan sheep, with horns quite erect, twisted like a screw, and beautifully furrowed on the outside. This kind is common in Hungary, and large flocks of them are found on Mount Ida, in Crete. The manners of this animal are naturally harmless and timid; it threatens by stamping with its foot, but its only resistance is by butting with its horns. It generally brings one young one at a time, sometimes two, and rarely three. It is a valuable animal to the farmer, as it is kept at the least expence of any, and will thrive upon almost any pasture ground, not particularly wet; a constant damp causes them to rot.

Mrs. HARCOURT.

Almost every part of it may be applied to some useful purpose. The flesh is a delicate and wholesome food. The skin, when dressed, forms different parts of our apparel, as shoes, and gloves; it is also used for covers of books. The entrails, properly prepared and twisted, are used in clocks, and various musical instruments. The bones calcined, form materials for tests for the refiner. The milk is thicker than that of cows, and consequently yields a greater quantity, in proportion, of butter and cheese: and even the dung is useful as a rich manure; but the most valuable part of all is the fleece, or wool, which when washed, shorn, dressed, combed, spun, and wove, makes a vast variety of stuffs and cloths, suitable both for cloathing and furniture, and was so highly valued by the ancients for its utility, as to have given rise to the story of the golden fleece, which I request the favour of Charles to relate.

CHARLES.

The ancients, always fond of fables, concealed the simplest events, under the appearance of some extraordinary story. Jason, son of AEson, king of Thessaly, sailed in the first large ship (called Argo) to fetch the golden fleece from Colchis. Fifty-four brave Thessalians accompanied him in his expedition, and from the name of the vessel are called Argonauts. Their object is supposed to have been the establishment of a profitable trade in wool, in which that country excelled. The difficulties he met with in his undertaking, and which he overcame by his prudence, are represented by the fable of a dragon, that guarded the fleece, and which he is said to have killed by the assistance of Medea, an enchantress. The education this prince had received from Chiron, the centaur, famous for his arts and learning, had fitted him for cultivating commerce, and promoting useful discoveries. Jason at length reigned, and died peaceably at Colchis.

SOPHIA.

Another proof of the high veneration that was paid to the inventors of the woollen manufacture, is, that the art of preparing it was attributed to Minerva, the goddess of wisdom, and the protectress of the useful arts.

CECILIA.

We have been entertained with the history of the sheep, and a general account of its uses; but I am very desirous of knowing the manner of working wool, and rendering so rough a material fit for the purpose of spinning and weaving fine cloth.

Mrs. HARCOURT.

Various are the operations it undergoes before it is in a proper state for the purpose you mention. The fleeces, when taken out of the bales in which they are packed, after shearing, must be scoured;

when the wool has continued long enough in the liquor to dissolve and loosen the grease, it is taken out, and well washed and dried; it is then beat with rods, on hurdles of wood, to clear it of the dust and grosser filth. The next thing is to pick it, and oil it with oil of olives. It is now given out to the spinners, who first card it on the knee; that is, pass it between the points or teeth of two instruments, something like a curry-comb, called cards, to disentangle it, and prepare it for spinning, which is an operation too common to need description. The thread or worsted being spun, reeled, and made into skeins, is ready for the hand of the weaver, who begins his work by putting the warp, or threads, the long way of the piece, into the loom, which he stiffens with size before he forms the woof, which is done by throwing the thread with a shuttle across the warp, till the work be finished; when it is to be cleared of all knots, &c. and carried to the fuller to be scoured and cleansed, ready for dying; after it is dyed, it is pressed and prepared for sale. Different kinds of goods require variation in the process, according to the kind of stuff intended to be made.

AUGUSTA.

Wool is applied to a vast many different purposes; what are the principal manufactures in which it is employed?

Mr. HARCOURT.

Let Henry endeavour to enumerate the things that we use, that are made of wool.

HENRY.

Broad cloths for men's coats, flannel, blankets, carpets, rugs, caps, stockings, and various kinds of stuffs.

CECILIA.

All stockings are not knitted, how are the other made?

Mr. HARCOURT.

They are wove in a machine, called a stocking-frame, very ingeniously contrived, but too complex to give you any idea of it by description. Wool is the staple commodity of this island, and forms the principal article in our foreign and domestic trade. The yearly produce of wool in England, towards the close of the last century, was calculated at two millions sterling, and consequently it gives employment to a vast number of hands. A pack, or two hundred and forty pounds weight of short wool, is computed to employ sixty-three persons a week, to manufacture it into cloths: and when it is made into stuffs or stockings, it employs a much greater number.

CHARLES.

The working of wool is doubtless an invention of great antiquity; but how long has it been introduced into England?

Mr. HARCOURT.

It may be said to have risen into notice about the fourteenth century. King Edward the third introduced the fine woollen manufacture from the Netherlands. Queen Elizabeth greatly improved the state of this manufacture by her patronage, in which she received considerable assistance from the troubles in the Low Countries, excited by the severity of the Duke of Alva, and the Spanish inquisition, on account of religion, which drove numbers of manufacturers to take shelter in England, where they enjoyed protection and encouragement to settle. Contrast the conduct of Elizabeth and the Duke of Alva. The one cherished the useful arts, and diffused happiness and wealth among her people; the other, from a gloomy superstition, deprived his country of useful manufacturers, and obliged them to take refuge in the dominions of his rival, which they enriched by their labours and skill.

Mrs. HARCOURT.

Nature is an excellent instructress. From the nautilus men learned the art of sailing. From the spider they are supposed to have been taught the art of weaving. Attention to natural objects will probably supply new discoveries, which are now unthought of.

CHARLES.

What country produces the finest wool?

Mr. HARCOURT.

The wool of Asia excels that of Europe. Of the European, none is more valued than the Spanish and the English. Spain is famous for its breed of sheep, they have frequently ten thousand in a flock, under the care of fifty shepherds, who are subservient to the authority of one man.

HENRY.

I think I should like to be a shepherd, it must be an easy pleasant life.

Mrs. HARCOURT.

They generally pass their time in a very indolent useless manner; though some in the north of England knit stockings, yet it appears to me, that a better plan of employment might be suggested for them, without interfering with their principal occupation. Those who could read and write, might keep a register of the weather, and make observations upon the natural objects that presented themselves to their view, which might be a means of promoting useful knowledge.

CHARLES.

Is it not the custom for the lord chancellor, the judges, and masters in chancery, to be seated on woolsacks, in the house of Lords?

Mr. HARCOURT.

That is a custom not very easy to be accounted for, unless it is to remind them of protecting and maintaining the woollen manufactures of this country.

Mrs. HARCOURT.

It is time to put an end to our conversation. Supper is ready. Good night, Children.

CONVERSATION 12

Mrs. HARCOURT.

A S the woollen manufacture seemed to afford us great entertainment the last time we met, may we not be amused with
the particulars of the linen and cotton manufactures in their various branches? Sophia has made herself acquainted with the natural
definitions of both flax and hemp, with the design of contributing
materials for our conversation.

Mr. HARCOURT.

We cannot adopt a more suitable subject; the one leads the way
to the other. In the early savage state, when men united in small
societies, for the sake of protection and defence, we find they
clothed themselves with the skins of beasts in their rough natural
state, unimproved by any art or dressing, merely for the purposes
of decency and warmth. In cold climates, the savage tribes frequently wear the hair inwards. As they advance to a higher state
of civilization, they make use of materials that admit of greater skill
in preparing, and study ornament as well as use. Captain Cook
relates, that the inhabitants of some places he visited, have a
method of weaving cloth of a certain species of grass. The natives
of Atooi make cloaks and caps of feathers, with great ingenuity, on
which they set a high value, and which appear appropriated to the
chiefs, and great men of the country. Many of the islands in the
South-Sea, are so far advanced towards civilized life, as to have an
established manufacture of cloth, which is made by the women.
They take the stalks or trunks of the paper-mulberry, which rarely
grows more than seven feet in height, and about the thickness of
four fingers. From these stalks they strip the bark, and scrape off
the exterior rinds after which the bark is rolled up, and softened
for some time in water; it is then beaten with a square instrument
of wood, full of coarse grooves, but sometimes with a plain one.
When sufficiently beaten, it is spread out to dry; the piece being
from four to six or seven feet in length, and about half as broad.
These pieces are joined by smearing part of them with the glutinous
juice of a berry, called Tooo; and, after being thus lengthened, they
are placed over a large piece of wood, with a sort of stamp,
composed of a fibrous substance laid beneath them. The manufacturers then take a bit of cloth, and having dipped it in a juice
expressed from the bark of a tree, called kokka, rub it briskly over

the piece that is making. This leaves a dry gloss, and a dull brown colour, upon the surface, and the stamp makes, at the same time, a slight impression, which finishes the work. But when we compare these simple works, with the variety, elegance, and utility of the manufactures of the polished nations of Europe and Asia, the degrees of refinement and civilization are clearly marked; and we are enabled to form distinct ideas of the difference between the rude productions of the untutored mind, and those which are the result of science and art; but I am wandering from our subject. Sophia, your young friends wait impatiently to hear your account of flax and hemp, which form the materials of the linen of this country, from the coarsest cloth, to the finest lace.

SOPHIA.

Flax is a genus of the pentandria, pentagynia classes. The flower has a permanent empalement, composed of five small spear-shaped acute leaves, five large oblong petals and five awl-shaped erect stamina, terminated by arrow-shaped summits. In the centre is situated an oval germin, supporting five slender styles, crowned by reflex stigmas, which turn to a globular capsule with ten cells, opening with five valves, in each cell is lodged one oval smooth seed, with an acute point. There are fourteen species. The common flax is an annual plant, that will grow in any kind of good sound land. The best land yields the best flax.

CHARLES.

As the tilling and ordering of flax is so profitable to the farmer, I regret it is not more frequently cultivated.

Mr. HARCOURT.

Since you seem to be acquainted with the management of it; pray tell us the seasons for sowing and gathering it.

CHARLES.

The time of sowing is the latter end of March. The best way of sowing flax-seed is to drill it in equidistant rows, about ten inches from one another. Towards the end of August the flax will begin to ripen, and must be pulled as soon as the seed grows brown, and bends down the heads.

Mr. HARCOURT.

Riga supplies us with the best seed. Scotland and Ireland import great quantities from thence annually. Flax and hemp have the remarkable property of communicating a poisonous quality to water, when laid in it for the purpose of decaying the stem, and procuring the bark for mechanical purposes, so that cattle die that drink of it.

AUGUSTA.

I am quite unacquainted with the manner of making linen from a plant. Mr. Harcourt said just now, that hemp and flax formed the materials of linen. I thought linen had been made of thread.

CECILIA.

So it is; but all the various sorts of thread we use are made of flax.

Mrs. HARCOURT.

Hemp is very similar to flax in its culture and use, therefore one description of the manner of preparing them will be sufficient for both. When they gather it, they pull it up by the roots, after which they bind it up in bundles. They comb out the heads on the teeth of a ripple, which pulls off the leaves, the husks of the seeds, and the seeds themselves together. These are gathered in a heap, and left in that condition for a few days, in order to heat a little, after which they are spread out to dry, before they are threshed, and the seeds are separated by winnowing and sifting. Then, in order to rot the bark, they are laid in water, that it may be more easily separated from the reed. When it is sufficiently rotted, the stalks are dried in an oven or kiln. The next thing to be done is peeling off the bark, which is performed by various means, but it is most expeditiously effected by mills.

HENRY.

Do not people beat hemp in Bridewell?

Mr. HARCOURT.

The beating hemp with beetles is a very laborious employment, and is used as a punishment for the idle and dissolute, who are confined there for small crimes.

93

Mrs. HARCOURT.

In order to complete the process, they beat it till it is soft and pliable, and, after washing and bleaching, it is heckled with instruments resembling a wool-dresser's comb, to disentangle the shorter tow from the longer, which is then fit to be spun into thread, for the different purposes of weaving, &c.

AUGUSTA.

I am ashamed of my ignorance; but it is wonderful to me, to think that this piece of linen ever grew in a field.

Mr. HARCOURT.

It is said that the first step to knowledge, is a consciousness of ignorance. Endeavour, children, to increase your stock of useful knowledge daily, by attention to everything you see and hear. There are various kinds of linen, the principal materials of which are flax, cotton, and hemp. The linen trade of Europe is chiefly in the hands of the Russians, Germans, Flemings, Hollanders, French, and Irish. Cotton is a woolly or downy substance, which incloses the seed, and is contained in a brown husk or seed vessel of a certain plant, that grows both in the East and West Indies. There are several species of this plant cultivated in different places. Cotton forms a very considerable article of commerce; it is distinguished into two sorts; cotton in the wool, and spun cotton. The first is quilted between two stuffs, and is made use of for the purpose of rendering them thick and warm, as for coverlids for beds, petticoats, &c. but the latter kind is of most general use, as when spun and wove, it makes calicoes, cloths, muslins, dimities, besides a kind of quilting, ingeniously contrived to resemble that done with a needle. It is also frequently intermixed with silk or flax, in the composition of various kinds of stuffs. Manchester, which has long been celebrated for various branches of the linen, silk, and cotton manufacture, is now conspicuous as the centre of the cotton trade.

CHARLES.

Cotton anciently grew only in Egypt; and was confined to the use of the priests and sacrificers, for a singular kind of gown, worn by them alone.

Mrs. HARCOURT.

Although hemp does not form a material for works of so delicate a texture as flax and cotton, it deserves to be noticed for the many useful properties it contains. Of what use would our ships be, without ropes and sails? Sophia, you have performed but half your promise; I call upon you now to fulfil the other part of your engagement.

SOPHIA.

I am always ready to obey you. Hemp is a species of the dioecia pentandria class. It is male and female in different plants. The male flowers have a five-leaved concave empalement, without petals, but have five short hairy stamina, terminated by oblong square summits. The female flowers have permanent empalements of one leaf, without petals, but a small germin, which afterwards becomes a globular depressed seed, inclosed in the empalement. We have but one species of this plant, which is propagated in the rich fenny parts of Lincolnshire, in great quantities for its bark, which is useful for cordage, cloth, &c.

CECILIA.

Oh, I remember, my uncle shewed me some, when I was on a visit at his house. It rises quick into a tall slender shrub, its stem is hollow, and he told me, was frequently made into charcoal, and is used in that form in the composition of gunpowder. Its leaves arise from the same pedicle, and are a little jagged, yielding a strong smell, apt to make one's head ach. The flowers grow in clusters, and the bark is a tissue of fibres, joined together by a soft matter, which easily rots away.

Mr. HARCOURT.

It does not appear that the ancients were acquainted with the use of hemp, with respect to the thread that it affords. The moderns are not contented with that production only, but torture this poor plant, for another valuable commodity that it contains; Henry can tell us what that is.

HENRY.

Oil: I have not forgotten what I saw at the mill. They bruise the seed of flax, which is called linseed, as well as hempseed, with vast hammers, which are too heavy for men to lift; and are set a going with wheels, which are turned by the stream of a river.

Mr. HARCOURT.

You shew a good memory. This oil has most of the qualities of the nut-oil, and is used as a substitute for it in painting. The oil drawn without the assistance of fire, is much esteemed in medicine, especially in the cure of catarrhs, coughs, asthmas, &c. After the oil is squeezed from the seeds, the seeds are heated over the fire, and being put into woollen bags, are pressed into pieces about twelve inches long, and six inches wide, called oil-cakes, and used to fatten cattle. These cakes, beaten again to dust, become an excellent manure for land. Thus ingenuity and industry have applied almost every part of this plant to a valuable purpose.

CHARLES.

There is still one kind of linen cloth that we have not mentioned, and which I think more curious and extraordinary than any that has been described. If Augusta is surprised that linen should be spun from the fibres of plants, how much more astonished will she be, to find that cloth has been made of stone?

AUGUSTA.

I am less inclined to disbelieve things that I do not understand, than I was, when first your kind mother permitted me to join in these instructive conversations; since I have heard many things equally new and wonderful to me, who had never been taught to observe or reflect upon the objects that fell in my way; but this time, Charles, I am really incredulous, and think you say this only to banter me.

CHARLES.

Nothing is more certain. I have seen and handled specimens of it; and to increase the wonder of my tale, this cloth will not consume in the fiercest fire.

CECILIA.

Pray, Charles, explain it. This is an enigma that we cannot guess.

CHARLES.

There is a mineral substance, called asbestos, of a whitish or silver colour, and a woolly texture, consisting of small threads or fibres, endued with the wonderful property of resisting fire, and remaining unconsumed in the intensest heat. A method has been found of working these fibres into cloth and paper. This kind of linen was much esteemed by the ancients, being held equally precious with the richest pearls. Pliny says, he had seen napkins made of it, which, when taken soiled from the table at a feast, were thrown into the fire, and were better scoured in that manner, than they could have been, if they had been washed in water; but the purpose, for which it was so highly valued, was the making of shrouds for royal funerals, to wrap up the corpse, so that the ashes of the deceased might be preserved distinct from those of the wood, &c. of which the funeral pile was composed. They also made the wicks of their perpetual lamps of the same material.

CECILIA.

Did not the ancients bury their dead in the same manner we do?

Mr. HARCOURT.

Different nations and ages have had various modes of disposing of their deceased friends and relations. The ancient Romans carried the body, borne on a bed or litter, covered with purple, and followed by the kindred of the deceased, to the rostra; and if he had been a person of great quality, attended by old women, called praeficae, singing songs in his praise; and the funeral was preceded by waxen images of all his predecessors borne on poles. When arrived there, the nearest of kin pronounced an oration extolling his virtues and those of his ancestors; after which they proceeded to the funeral pile, whereupon they laid the body, and set fire to the whole. The ashes were then carefully gathered up, and inclosed in an urn, which was placed in the sepulchre or tomb. The ceremonies of the Egyptians were very peculiar. They embalmed the body with aromatic spices and perfumes, in order to preserve it from decay; and it is supposed that the pyramids, so wonderful for their antiquity and magnitude, were erected as monuments or tombs to contain the bodies of their departed kings.

Mrs. HARCOURT.

One of their customs pleases me much, as I think it was calculated to restrain vice, and encourage virtue. They brought their
kings to a form of trial after their death; those who were convicted
of having oppressed their people, and leading bad lives, were
deprived of the honours of burial, and their memories held in
detestation; but every respect was paid to those who had passed
their lives in a virtuous manner; and even durable monuments
erected to perpetuate their names, and transmit the recollection of
their example to the latest posterity. To-morrow evening we shall
select the silk manufacture as a subject, well suited to follow those
of wool and linen, and forming a proper sequel to them. At present
I find myself a little indisposed, and wish to retire early. Adieu, my
dear children, easy dreams, and a good night to you.

CONVERSATION 13

Mrs. HARCOURT.

ACCORDING to our agreement yesterday, we shall pursue the manufacture of silk through its various operations this evening; but as many of these are very similar to the same processes, in those of flax and hemp, we shall only just mention them, and dwell more on the manners and metamorphoses of the minute labourer, whose skill supplies the finest palaces with their richest furniture, and without whose aid the habits of queens and princesses would be coarse and mean.

Mr. HARCOURT.

Wool and flax are extremely valuable for their use, and are no more to be contemned in comparing them with silk, than iron is to be undervalued in comparison with gold and silver. The coarser metal, like the coarser materials for cloth or stuff, is far more necessary for our accommodation, though less brilliant and inferior for the purposes of ornament and splendour, than the more beautiful productions of the mine or the silk-worm. Diamonds are dazzling to the eyes of the superficial observer, but was their real value subtracted from the adventitious price, that the refinement and luxury have raised them to, we, like the cock in the fable, should prefer something more useful, and less shining.

CHARLES.

I cannot help remarking, how sparing nature has been in those productions that are not of essential use, though highly prized, and sought with great avidity by the avarice of man.

Mr. HARCOURT.

Nature, wise in all her ways, has bestowed the most useful things in the greatest abundance; and in many instances, has rendered those objects, which we are apt to despise for their minuteness and apparent insignificancy, or because they are so common, that they do not call forth our attention, the most necessary to our subsistence and convenience.

Mrs. HARCOURT.

The ancients were but little acquainted with the use and manufacture of the very soft, fine, bright, delicate thread, produced by the silk-worm. It was a very scarce commodity among them for many ages. The art of manufacturing it was first invented in the isle of Cos: and Pamphila, daughter of Platis, is honoured as the inventress.

CHARLES.

It was not long unknown to the Romans, although it was so rare, that it was even sold weight for weight with gold. And I have read that the emperor Aurelian, who died in the year 275, refused the empress, his wife, a suit of silk, which she solicited of him with much earnestness, merely on account of its dearness. Heliogabalus, the emperor, who died about half a century before Aurelian, is said to be the first person who wore a holosericum, or garment all of silk.

Mr. HARCOURT.

The Greeks of Alexander the Great's army, are supposed to have brought wrought silk first from Persia, into Greece, about three hundred and twenty-three years before Christ. But the manufacture of it was confined to Phoenicia, from whence it was dispersed over the West. Two monks, coming from the Indies to Constantinople, in 555, under the patronage of the Emperor Justinian, brought with them great quantities of silk-worms; with instructions for the hatching their eggs, rearing and feeding the worms, and spinning and working the silk; which was the means of establishing manufactures at Athens, Thebes, and Corinth. The Venetians, soon after this time, commencing a commerce with the Greek empire, supplied all the western parts of Europe with silks for many centuries. But various improvements have been made in the art since that time; such as damasks, velvets, &c. The rest of Italy and Spain, by degrees, learned this art, from some manufactories established by Roger the Second, King of Sicily, about 1150, in different parts of his dominions. And a little before the reign of Francis the First, the French became masters of it.

SOPHIA.

There was a company of silk women in England so early as the year 1455.

Mrs. HARCOURT.

It is most probable that they were only employed in needle-work of silk and thread; for Italy supplied England with the broad manufacture, the chief part of the fifteenth century.

Mr. HARCOURT.

Silk remained a rarity a long time in France. Their king, Henry the Second, is supposed to have worn the first pair of knit silk-stockings. After the civil wars, the plantations of mulberry-trees were greatly encouraged by Henry the Fourth, surnamed the Great, on account of the love he shewed his people, and the true patriotism he displayed during his troublesome reign. His succes-sors continued to patronise the culture of these trees, and the produce of silk is at this day very considerable in that country. King James the First was very earnest to introduce it into England, but unhappily without effect. Although we have hitherto failed in rearing the worms, and raising raw silk of our own, the broad silk manufacture was introduced among us as early as the year 1620, and pursued with great vigour and advantage.

Mrs. HARCOURT.

Greatly were we indebted to the tyranny and intolerance of our neighbours, the French, who by the revocation of the edict of Nantes, in 1685, which means the repealing a law made in favour of Protestants, drove vast numbers of their most skilful workmen in this branch, to take shelter in our land of liberty; they were kindly received, and settled in Spital-Fields, where they have carried on an ingenious and flourishing manufacture, till within these few years, that the British ladies have exchanged the wear of silk, for that of calicoes and muslins, by which transition these poor manu-facturers are reduced to a very distressed situation; being without employment, and in want of most of the necessaries of life. It is an object worthy the consideration of persons of ability, to suggest some plan for turning the industry of so many hands into a different channel, and rendering them capable of maintaining their families, and becoming again useful to society. The silkworm is an insect, not more remarkable for the precious matter it furnishes, than for the many forms it assumes. Cecilia, who keeps many of them, will amuse us with an account of these metamorphoses.

101

CECILIA.

From an egg, about the size of a pin's head, it becomes a small black worm, which daily increases, till it is as large as a common caterpillar; during its worm state, it frequently changes its skin, and becomes by degrees of a light ash colour, inclined to yellow, and almost transparent when about to spin. Henry brings me fresh mulberry leaves every morning to feed them with. When come to maturity, the silk-worm winds itself up in a silken bag or case, about the size and shape of a pigeon's egg; it forms this ball, by moving its mouth backwards and forwards, chusing some corner to begin its work in, and fastening its silk, with a kind of natural gum, to the sides, till it has entirely inclosed itself: always working from one single end, which it never breaks, unless disturbed; and it is so fine, and so long, that I have read, that those who have examined it attentively, think they speak within compass, when they affirm, that each ball contains silk enough to reach the length of six English miles. On opening this curious web, one is surprised to find a chrysalis or aurelia, instead of a silk-worm, which is brown, and about the size of a bean. In this state it remains for some time apparently without life or motion; till at length out creeps a whitish moth, leaving the husk or outer skin of the chrysalis behind it. This is the last form it assumes; for, after having laid a multitude of eggs, it dies, and leaves them to be hatched by the warmth of the succeeding spring.

Mrs. HARCOURT.

When the worm is supposed to have finished its work, which is generally in about ten days: the people who are employed in the care of these insects, for the sake of profit, collect the golden balls from off the mulberry trees, to the leaves of which they glue their silk, and putting a handful of them into a copper of warm water, of a proper temperature to dissolve the gum, and occasion the silk to wind off more readily, having first pulled off a woolly coarse kind of silk, which covers the balls. They take the ends of twelve or fourteen cones at a time, and wind them off into skeins. In order to prepare this beautiful material for the hand of the weaver, to be wrought into silks, stuffs, brocades, satins, velvets, ribbons, gauzes, &c. it is spun, reeled, milled, bleached, and dyed in a manner so similar to other materials, as to render a particular description unnecessary.

Mr. HARCOURT.

There is a kind of silk, that we must not omit mentioning, which comes from the East-Indies, and is not the work of the silk-worm, but comes from a plant, that produces it in pods, much like those of the cotton-tree. The matter this pod contains is extremely white, fine, and moderately glossy. It spins easily, and is used in several manufactures of Indian and Chinese stuffs.

SOPHIA.

I think I have heard of silk being spun from cobwebs.

AUGUSTA.

Surely that would be impossible, the threads are so fine and slender; besides, who would be willing to breed and tend spiders. I am terrified at the sight of one. How frightful would it be to enter a room where thousands were confined! I shudder at the thought.

Mrs. HARCOURT.

Had you not unfortunately been brought up with this prejudice, you would have had no more fear of a spider, than any other insect. In this country they are harmless, and have far more reason to dread us, than we have to be apprehensive of them. Use your reason, overcome such groundless fears; with men of sense, they lay our sex under the imputation of affectation or ignorance, and savour strongly of vulgarity, and want of education. When you have attentively considered the curious structure of this insect, and how wonderfully every part is adapted to its intended purpose, I believe you will be more inclined to look at it, in future, with an eye of admiration than terror.

Mr. HARCOURT.

The secret has been discovered in France, within a few years, of procuring and preparing silk from spiders' webs, and the using it in several manufactures has been attempted. Spiders are distinguished by naturalists into several kinds, according to the construction of their parts; but with regard to the silk spiders, they are reduced to two kinds, those with long legs, and those with short, which last furnish the finest raw silk. The silk it makes is nearly as beautiful, glossy, and strong, as that of the silk-worm; the silk proceeds from five papilla or nipples, placed under the belly, towards the end of the tail. These serve as so many wire-drawing

103

irons, to form and mould a viscous liquor, which, when dried in the air, as it is drawn through them, forms the silk. The threads are of two kinds; the first is weak, and only serves for that kind of web, with which they catch flies. The second is much stronger, and is applied to wrap up their eggs in, which by means of this inclosure, are sheltered from the cold, and the depredations of other insects. They wind these threads very loosely round the eggs, resembling the balls or bags of silk-worms, that have been prepared and loosened for the distaff. After having gathered twelve or thirteen ounces of these bags, M. Bon, the person who made these experiments, had them well beaten for some time, to get out all the dust; he then washed them in lukewarm water; after this he steeped them in a large vessel, with soap, salt-petre, and gum arabic; when he boiled the whole, for three hours, over a gentle fire; the soap was then washed out of them, and the bags dried, to fit them for carding. Stockings and gloves were made of it, and presented to the Academy in Paris, as well as to our Royal Society in London. The great difficulty that remains to be surmounted, is the art of breeding and confining these voracious insects in a room together, as the natural fierceness of spiders renders them incapable of living in community. Four or five thousand, being distributed into cells, the large ones soon killed and devoured the smaller, so that, in a short time, there was left scarcely more than one or two in a cell; and to this apparent unnatural propensity of eating one another, the scarcity of spiders is attributed, considering the vast number of eggs they lay. Every spider lays six or seven hundred. The young ones live ten or twelve months without eating, and continue in their bags without growing, till the warmth of the returning summer, putting their viscid juices in motion, induces them to come forth, spin, and run about in search of food. But I believe Sophia is better qualified to give us a lecture on the construction and manners of this extraordinary little creature.

SOPHIA.

With peculiar pleasure I shall relate what particulars I am acquainted with, as I am convinced, no one, who has examined its parts with a microscope, can behold it again as an object of abhorrence. Spider, a genus of the aptera order of insects; Linnaeus enumerates forty-seven species. This insect affords, to the sagacious observer, a great many curious particulars. As the fly (which is the spider's natural prey) is an animal extremely cautious and nimble, and usually comes from above, it was necessary the spider should be furnished with a quick sight, and an ability of looking upwards, forwards, and sideways at the same time; and the microscope shews that the number, structure, and disposition of its eyes are wonderfully adapted to the serving all these purposes. Most spiders have eight eyes, two on the top of the head or body; for there is no division between them, the spider having no neck. These look directly upwards. There are two more in front, placed a little below these, and discovering all that passes forwards: and on each side, a couple more, one of which points sideways forwards, the other sideways backwards, so that it can see almost quite round. Whatever be the number of the spider's eyes, for there are not the same number in all the different species, they are, however, always immoveable and transparent, and are situated in a most curious manner. All spiders have eight legs, which they employ in walking, and two shorter ones, called arms, used in seizing their prey. All the legs are thickly beset with hairs, each has six joints, and ends with two hooked claws, which are jagged on the inside. By means of this sort of teeth in the claws, they seize very fast hold of their prey; besides these weapons of attack, nature has furnished this creature with a pair of sharp-crooked claws, or forceps, in the forepart of its head. These are placed horizontally or crosswise, and when not exerted for use, are concealed in two cases, contrived for their reception, in which they fold like a clasp knife, and there lie between two rows of teeth, which are likewise employed to hold fast the prey, so that a poor fly has not the least chance of escaping the jaws of such a well-armed formidable enemy.

HENRY.

Pray, mamma, lend me your microscope, that I may examine every spider I find.

Mrs. HARCOURT.

You are welcome to the use of it, provided you are careful not to break it. Mr. Lewenhoek, who has made microscopic objects his peculiar study, has computed, that one hundred of the single threads of a full-grown spider, are not equal to the diameter of the hair of his beard; and consequently, if the threads and hair be both round, ten thousand such threads are not bigger than such a hair. He calculates that when young spiders first begin to spin, four hundred of their threads are not larger than one, which is of a full growth. Allowing this to be fairly stated, four millions of a young spider's threads are not so big as the single hair of a man's beard.

AUGUSTA.

Astonishing minuteness! Since you say it is ridiculous, I will endeavour to overcome my aversion to spiders.

Mrs. HARCOURT.

We are going from home for a few weeks; by the time we meet again, I flatter myself you will have availed yourself of my advice on many subjects; and that I shall find you improved by the exertion of your reason, in the correction of any foibles you may have. Your young friends will think the separation tedious, but you will enjoy each other's company the more for this little interruption. Adieu, my dear child, may you enjoy health and happiness till our next meeting.

CONVERSATION 14

Mrs. HARCOURT.

I PARTICIPATE the general pleasure at being again assembled, after so long an absence, to renew those pleasing and instructive conversations, in which we have passed so many agreeable evenings. During our separation, our time has not been spent idly; we have attentively examined the different objects we have met with on our journey; and each one of us has collected observations on some particular subject, in order to furnish materials for new entertainment. My dear Augusta, how have you amused yourself since we have been absent? Have you added to your stock of knowledge by fresh acquisitions; or have you employed your time in perfecting yourself in those branches of science already begun?

AUGUSTA.

No one has so much reason to rejoice at your return, my dear Mrs. Harcourt, as myself. I have indeed deeply lamented your absence; for without a guide, or a companion, what pleasure is there in pursuing improvement? Summer is a season that tempts one abroad. I have walked a great deal, and in some of my rambles have availed myself of your directions, to become acquainted with the nature of plants and flowers. I have learned the names of the different parts that compose them; and, if Sophia will give me her kind assistance, I hope in time to become a botanist.

SOPHIA.

You cannot propose any thing more agreeable to me, than that we should pursue this delightful study together. Our walks will become more interesting, by having a particular object in view; every step we advance will supply new entertainment; from the humble moss, that creeps upon the thatch, to the stately oak, that adorns the forest.

CHARLES.

Gently, Sophia; you must not intrude upon the subject I have chosen. The humble moss, and its diminutive companions, I willingly relinquish to your claims; but the stately oak, and its attendant forest trees I have selected, as suitable to amuse this company with; and though I readily resign any thing to you that merely concerns myself, I cannot give up the only theme that I am prepared to speak upon.

SOPHIA.

Lay aside your apprehensions, brother; I shall have too much pleasure in hearing you explain their properties and uses, to desire to interrupt you; if my father has not provided any thing for this evening, may we not be favoured with your observations? I dare say we are all desirous of hearing them.

Mr. HARCOURT.

Charles has made so good a choice, that you cannot be more agreeably amused, than by attending to what he has collected on this subject. The beauty and utility of forest trees are so obvious and striking, that the most careless eye must be sensible of them. Charles, begin by telling us which are the principal trees used for timber.

CHARLES.

Oak, elm, ash, beech, poplar, walnut, chestnut, fir, and service tree; but they all yield to the oak, as well in beauty of foliage, as in the utility and duration of its timber. This noble tree forms our navies and cities; and, should the cultivation of it be neglected, we may vainly deplore the loss of those wooden walls, that have so long been our pride and defence.

HENRY.

I do not understand what you mean by that expression. I thought walls had always been built of brick or stone.

CHARLES.

I ask pardon for making use of a figurative term. The naval strength of our island is frequently called its wooden walls, and consequently depends very much upon the cultivation of the best species of timber. Every part of the oak has its use; the body is sawed into planks, to build ships and houses with; shingles, pales, laths, cooper's work, and wainscot, are made of oak; its wood is the most excellent for all works that require strength and duration. The bark is used by the tanner and dyer, to whom the very saw-dust is useful. The ashes and lye are made use of for bucking of linen, and to cleanse and purify wine. The roots are suitable to make handles for daggers, knives, &c. Its fruit, the acorn, supplies food for deer and hogs; and when bruised, all kinds of poultry will thrive on it. Man, before the cultivation of corn, fed on acorns, and in times of scarcity, they may still prove a valuable substitute. Different parts of the oak are used in medicine; they are all of an astringent, binding quality. The wood of this tree is the least adapted to works that require to be glued together, as it will not easily adhere, either with its own kind or any other wood.

CECILIA.

Is not ink made of oak galls? What part of the tree are they?

CHARLES.

Yes, they are used in making ink, as well as in the composition of various medicines; neither the oak apples nor the galls are any part of the tree; they are formed by insects, which deposit their eggs in the stem or leaf. There are various kinds of galls, formed by different insects, the inhabitants of a great variety of trees and shrubs.

Mrs. HARCOURT.

The history of galls is so curious, that I cannot resist relating some particulars concerning them. Among the smaller insects, there are many which, either in the whole state of the worm, or during some of the changes they undergo, are of so tender and delicate a structure, that they cannot bear the contact of air; and others that are continually exposed to the ravage of a number of destroyers. Provident nature, in order to their preservation, has allotted them the galls of trees and plants for an habitation; instinct directs them to make them for themselves; for they never find these excrescences ready formed. Some of these insects are produced from eggs, laid by their parent animal on the stalks of leaves, and as soon as they are hatched, make their way into the leaf or stalk, and find a safe lodging in this recess, and suitable food in its juices. Others are inserted by the mother fly, even in the egg state, within the substance of the trees and branches. The parents of these are a peculiar race of flies, supplied with an instrument at the end of their tails adapted to this purpose.

109

CECILIA.

How wonderful is the order of nature! the formation of the smallest insect, did we but know the purpose of its different parts, would furnish us with subject of admiration.

Mrs. HARCOURT.

The galls produced by different insects have a very different internal structure; some of them have only one large cavity, in which a number of the animals live in community; others have several small cavities, with communications between each; and others have different numbers of little cellules each separate; and finally, there are others in which there is only one cavity inhabited by one insect. The inhabitants of these two last kinds live in perfect solitude during the worm state, and can have no knowledge of any other living creature, till they have passed through the intermediate state of chrysalis, and become winged animals, like those to which they owed their origin, and are ready in their turn to lay their eggs, and provide for the security of their future offspring. The variations in the different kinds of galls are not confined to their structure merely; each species has its peculiarity. Some of them are so hard, that they equal the hardness of the wood they grow upon; and when cut open, appear composed of films much more densely and closely arranged than those of the wood itself; others are soft and spongy, and resemble some of the tender fruits in appearance. The first kind are called gall-nuts; and the latter apple-galls, or berry-galls; many of them are beautifully coloured, and are very useful to the dyer, as well as the physician. The kermes is the most valuable of them all, and produces a scarlet dye, which is more durable than brilliant; it would take up too much time to mention the various particulars of each species. Charles, resume the subject of the oak.

CHARLES.

There are many varieties of this useful tree, the different parts of each are capable of being turned to some advantage. Cork is the bark of a species of the holm oak. It grows in great abundance in Spain, Italy, France, &c. Depriving this tree of its bark does not injure it, for if timely care be not taken to strip it off, it splits and peels off of itself, being pushed up by another bark formed underneath. In order to prepare it for use, it is piled in heaps, in ponds or ditches, then flattened with weights, and dried. It is principally applied to purposes, to which its peculiar quality of repelling moisture is adapted; such as soles for shoes, corks for bottles, and bungs for barrels. Waistcoats for swimming have also been made of it; its excessive lightness rendering it suitable for the purpose, as well as its power of repelling the water.

Mr. HARCOURT.

The bark, or exterior covering of trees, is not only useful to man for various purposes, but it is formed for the preservation of the trees also; it defends them from external injury, and preserves them from the cold, when it is too severe for their tender bodies. The reason that evergreens retain their leaves during the rigours of winter, is, because their barks are of a more oily quality than the bark of other trees. There are a great many kinds of barks in use in the several arts. They are considered as powerful restoratives and strengtheners in medicine. The bark of the alder is used in dying; that of a peculiar species of birch is converted by the Indians into canoes, capable of holding twenty persons. A kind of rope is made of the bark of willows and linden-trees. The bark of the cocoa-tree forms the cordage of the Siamese, and most of the Asiatic and African nations. In the East-Indies they manufacture the bark of a certain tree into a kind of stuff or cloth; it is spun and dressed much after the manner of hemp: indeed flax and hemp, with all their toughness, are only the sap-vessels, or ligneous films of the bark of those plants. The East-Indian thread, produced from bark, is of a middle kind between silk and common thread; they sometimes manufacture it alone, as others mix it with silk, as in ginghams, &c.

SOPHIA.

The ancients wrote their books on bark, before the invention of paper, particularly on those of the ash and lilia, or lime-tree. The outer bark was not suitable for this purpose, they made use of the inner and finer, called phylyra.

Mr. HARCOURT.

And so durable was its texture, that there are manuscripts written on it still extant, a thousand years old. Bark is also service-able as a manure.

111

HENRY.

Papa, I think you told me some time ago, that birdlime was made of the bark of the holly.

Mr. HARCOURT.

Good boy, for remembering what you have been told; the usual method of preparing it, is by boiling it a sufficient time; the roots of hyacinths, asphodel, narcissus, and the black bryony, afford a tough stringy juice, in great quantities, of the same kind.

Mrs. HARCOURT.

I hope my Henry remembers also, that when he was told what materials composed birdlime, he was taught to despise its use. It is mean and unmanly to deprive a poor bird of its liberty, merely to gratify our inclinations, without being able to improve the condition of the little sufferer. And it is to be feared that, when naughty, thoughtless boys have smeared the boughs with this substance, they have sometimes forgotten to return to the place, and release the entangled prisoner, which, by their cruel neglect and carelessness, has been left to starve.

CECILIA.

And it would be still more piteous, was that prisoner a parent bird; its innocent little nestlings must suffer also a lingering death.

AUGUSTA.

My brothers have used birdlime, and set traps, without reflecting on the tortures they may have inflicted. I will repeat to them this conversation, and I am persuaded their hearts are too generous ever to be guilty of the same cruelty again.

CHARLES.

I shall next mention the elm, as second to the oak in size and beauty. It is particularly adapted to bear extremes of wet and dry, and therefore is frequently used for water-works, mills, pipes, pumps, aqueducts, &c. It is also suited to the purposes of the wheelwright. The fineness of its grain renders it fit for works of ornament such as foliages, &c. In times of scarcity, when hay and fodder have been difficult to obtain, the dried leaves of the elm

112

have been substituted as food for cattle. Charcoal made of elm is inferior to none but that of oak.

SOPHIA.

If charcoal be made of wood, what process is used to transform it to that state?

Mr. HARCOURT.

They begin the operation by clearing a circular piece of ground, of turf and other combustible matter. This space is filled with wood cut into pieces of about three feet in length, and laid in the form of a pile, with a stake driven into the centre; the whole is covered over moderately thick with turf and other rubbish; after setting up a moveable screen against the wind, the stake is pulled up, and the pile set on fire, by pouring well-kindled coals into the cavity. The wood chars without being consumed, by properly regulating the vent-holes, and keeping the mass covered. It is chiefly useful, where a clear strong fire, without smoke, is required. Mathematical instrument makers, engravers, &c. find charcoal very serviceable in polishing brass or copper-plates, after they have rubbed them clean with powdered pumice-stone. Charcoal and soot-black supply the painter and varnisher with the best and most durable black. One of the principal ingredients in making gunpowder is charcoal; but I do not mention this as an instance of its utility; happy would it be for mankind, did peace and good will prevail among them so powerfully, as to render such destructive inventions useless; but since this benign desire for universal harmony cannot be accomplished by the wishes of any one weak mortal, let each individual contribute his share towards preserving private peace, by subduing and regulating his angry passions; and cultivating and improving his benevolent dispositions.

Mrs. HARCOURT.

You have omitted to mention the baneful effects of the fume of charcoal; there have been many instances of persons who have been shut up in close rooms with charcoal fires in them, that have been found dead in a few hours. Charles, you must bear our interruptions with patience, you are now at liberty to proceed.

CHARLES.

I consider them as valuable additions to the few observations I have been able to collect; nor could I go on, unless you and my father will condescend to assist me. The ash, next to the oak, is of most universal use; it serves the soldier for spears, the carpenter, wheelwright, and cartwright for ploughs, axle-trees, wheel-rings, harrows, and oars. It is useful to the turner, cooper, and thatcher, and is superior to all other kinds for garden palisades, hop-yards, poles, and spars.

HENRY.

You told us that ships were built of oak; but I cannot think that the body of an oak, is either tall or straight enough to make the masts.

CHARLES.

The masts are made of fir or pine, which are tall, straight trees, adapted to the purpose; they love a chalky soil, and thrive well in a cold climate. Norway produces them in great abundance; they form that kind of timber commonly called deal, which is so much in use for floors, wainscots, &c. It is supposed that the enormous wooden horse, introduced by the artifice of Ulysses within the walls of Troy, and which was the means of destroying that famous city, after sustaining a siege of ten years, was formed of this tree.

Mr. HARCOURT.

The pine and fir trees are not valuable for their timber only, but turpentine, pitch, rosin and tar are made from them by the following simple process. In the spring, when the sap runs most freely, they pare off the bark of the pine-tree, and cut a hole at the bottom to receive the sap; as it runs down, it leaves a white matter, rather thicker than cream, which is substituted instead of white wax, in the making of flambeaux. The liquor that runs into the hole at the bottom, is ladled into a large basket; great part of this immediately runs through into stone or earthen pots, prepared to receive it, and forms the common turpentine. The thicker matter, which remains in the basket, is distilled with a large quantity of water, as long as any oil is seen swimming upon the surface of the water; which when skimmed off, is common oil, or spirit of turpentine. The matter, that settles at the bottom of the still, is yellow rosin. When they have obtained all they can from the sap of the tree, they cut it

114

down, and hew the wood into billets, with which they fill a pit dug in the earth, and then set them on fire; whilst burning, there runs from them a black thick matter, which is tar; if they desire to make it into pitch, they boil it without adding any thing to it, and the work is completed. Charles, continue your account.

CHARLES.

The turner uses the wood of the beech-tree for dishes, trays, rims for buckets, trenchers, &c. The upholsterer forms it into chairs, stools, bedsteads, bellows, &c. The bark is used for floats for fishing nets, instead of cork. It is very subject to the worm, which unfits it for purposes, where duration is requisite; but various parts of it are applied successfully to lighter uses. Bandboxes, scabbards for swords, and hat-cases are made of the thin lamina, or scale of this tree, and then covered with thin leather or paper. The mast or fruit fattens deer and swine; squirrels, mice, and dormice greedily devour the kernels of the mast; and some of our most favourite singing-birds; such as thrushes, blackbirds, &c., are preserved by them during the season that other food is scarce. The leaves, which afford an agreeable shade from the rays of the sun in summer, make the best and easiest mattresses, if gathered in autumn. Walnut is valued by the joiner and cabinet-maker for its beautiful variations of colour and grain, and is used in inlaid works.

Mrs. HARCOURT.

Of late years the drawing-rooms of people of fashion have been furnished with tables curiously inlaid with wood of various kinds, and the use of mahogany much laid aside. This gives scope for the exercise of taste in the artist, who, when at a loss for a colour in the natural wood, suited to his purpose, unites the art of colouring or staining it to that of design; festoons of flowers, fruits, birds, &c. admirably executed, decorate the chairs and other pieces of furniture, in the place of the heavy gilding that adorned the state rooms of our ancestors, who were more delighted with magnificence than elegance. The art of japanning and varnishing, which is now greatly improved, adds much to the beauty of painted or coloured wood. Substantial mahogany furniture is best suited to people whose rank and fortune subject them to the rules of useful economy, and whose duty it is to prefer utility to splendour and show. Sophia, do you recollect what country produces that species of cedar, the wood of which we call mahogany?

115

SOPHIA.

It is a native of the warmest parts of America, abounding in the islands of Cuba, Jamaica, and Hispaniola.

CHARLES.

There are many species of the cedar-tree; they were highly valued by the ancients for their durability and beauty. Solomon's temple and palace were both built with it, which is a mark of its high estimation. They grow to a very great size, and thrive best in a poor soil. The chestnut-trees that grow out of the lava of Mount Etna, in the island of Sicily, exceed any that I have heard of in magnitude. The agreeable traveller, Brydone,* relates, that the most celebrated among these, is called the castagno de cento cavalli; and that it measures two hundred and four feet round, though said to be united below in one stem, and is a mighty bush of five large trees growing together. The hollow of one of these is supposed to contain one hundred sheep.

Mr. HARCOURT.

Woods and groves were held sacred through all antiquity. The Pagans generally built their temples in or near them, and the druids and bards, who were the ministers of religion among the ancient Britons, held them in the highest veneration. Particular trees were frequently consecrated among the heathens to some favourite divinity. The laurel was devoted to Apollo, who presided over poetry and the fine arts; hence victors in the Olympic games, successful poets, and conquering heroes have been rewarded with crowns of laurel. The myrtle was the favourite tree of Venus, and the vine appropriated to Bacchus. White poplar was used in the sacrifices to Jupiter, and the pine on the alter of Ceres. The Persian Magi burned their sacrifices with myrtle and boughs of laurel. The mythology of the Pagans extended the idea of the tutelary protection of woods and groves so far, as to believe that they were generally inhabited by dryads, or wood nymphs.

---

* Patrick Brydone's popular epistolary *Tour through Sicily and Malta* (1773) was issued in many editions during the late 18th century. Priscilla Wakefield, an armchair traveller, drew upon Brydone's book for her own travel books.

Mrs. HARCOURT.

I am not surprised that minds uninstructed in the principles of true religion, impressed only by enthusiastic notions of the Deity, should be affected by the appearance of awe and solemnity that is felt on entering a thick impervious shade. Milton, in his Il Penseroso, seems sensible of the alliance between the gloom of a tall forest and melancholy enthusiasm. He says:

Me, Goddess, bring
To arched walks of twilight groves,
And shadows brown that Sylvan loves,
Of pine, or monumental oak,
Where the rude axe with heavy stroke
Was never heard the Nymphs to daunt,
Or fright them from their hallow'd haunt;
There in close covert, by some brook
where no profaner eye may look,
Hide me from day's garish eye, &c.

CHARLES.

At the time of the Norman conquest, and for many years after, prodigious tracts of land in this island remained covered with forest trees and underwood; they were not suffered to be cleared for the purposes of cultivation, lest the game, which took shelter in them, should be destroyed. Hunting was a favourite diversion with the kings and great men of that age, and they unfeelingly sacrificed the public welfare to their own private gratifications.

Mr. HARCOURT.

As the number of inhabitants increased, agriculture gradually improved; the great power of the barons being diminished, the people at large became of more consequence, and it was found necessary to listen to their importunity, and convert some of these extensive royal forests into smiling corn-fields, the harbingers of comfort and plenty. It will be happy if the present generation do not run into the opposite extreme, and by neglecting the planting and preserving of timber, subject this country to the inconvenience and disadvantage of being supplied from a foreign market. Indolence, the love of present advantage, and want of attention to the good of posterity, are obstacles to the improvement and practice of this useful part of husbandry. Country gentlemen of fortune, who have leisure and money to advance, can hardly render their country a more acceptable service, than by raising valuable plantations of the best kinds of timber for the use of succeeding generations. Their reward must consist in the patriotism and benevolence of their intentions, and in the increasing value of their estates, as the period of the life of man gives no expectation of the planter enjoying the fruit of his own labour: an oak not arriving at perfection much short of a century. Charles, you must oblige us with a further account of this interesting subject to-morrow evening; the time of separation is arrived. Adieu, my dear children.

CONVERSATION 15

On Forest Trees, continued.

AUGUSTA.

I HOPE I am not come too soon, I was so impatient to hear a continuation of last night's conversation, that I hastened tea, in order to be here early.

Mrs. HARCOURT.

The same inclination seems to have drawn each of us here rather earlier than usual; a pleasing assurance, that our lectures are not tedious, but that our attendance is rather voluntary than forced.

Mr. HARCOURT.

Instruction should always be rendered agreeable, in order to be beneficial to those that are to learn. The skill of a preceptor consists in gaining the affections of his pupils, and conveying knowledge in so gradual and clear a manner, as to adapt it to the strength of the young student's capacity. Many a poor child has been disgusted with books and learning, by the heavy laborious tasks that have been given him to learn by heart, before he was capable of understanding them. The spirit of improvement, that distinguishes this enlightened age, shines in nothing more conspicuously than in education. Persons of genius have not thought it unworthy of their talents to compose books purposely for the instruction of the infant mind, and various ingenious methods of facilitating the acquisition of knowledge have been invented.

Mrs. HARCOURT.

The austere manners of former times secluded children from the advantage of conversing with their parents or instructors; an unnatural distance was maintained between them; they were seldom admitted into the parlour, but to pay a ceremonious visit. The great Duke of Sully relates, in his Memoirs, that his children were never suffered to sit at table in his presence on chairs with backs to them. The times are greatly altered in this respect for the better, and the familiar intercourse, that is now maintained with young people by their parents, and those who preside over their education, affords them an agreeable opportunity of enlarging their minds, and at-

119

taining a fund of knowledge, by the easy medium of conversation. The liberality, with which young persons are treated in the present times, promises still greater hopes of advantage in the culture of the heart and disposition, than in the improvement of the faculties; by substituting real affection and friendship, in lieu of that distant respect, which is only the shadow of it.

SOPHIA.

I flatter myself, that there is not one of us, that is insensible to the privileges we enjoy, by the indulgence of our kind parents; particularly that of being permitted, nay, encouraged to open our whole bosoms to them.

AUGUSTA.

Forgive me, if I almost envy you this unspeakable comfort; deprived of a mother, before I was capable of knowing my loss, I have been a stranger to those tender sensations, that unite the heart of a child to so dear a connection. My father, though extremely fond of me, is often obliged to leave me for months together, on account of business, to the care of a governess that I cannot love; had I been so fortunate as to have been placed under such a woman as your Mrs. Selwyn, who treats you with kindness, is never angry without cause, and spares no pains for your improvement, I think I should have regarded her as an adopted mother, and loved her with equal tenderness; but the caprice, ill-humour, and indolence of Mrs. Marchment discourage me from endeavouring to please her; and had it not been for the compassionate attention of my dear Mrs. Harcourt, I must ever have remained ignorant and self-conceited, confirmed in error, a slave to bad habits, and my unsubdued passions.

Mrs. HARCOURT.

Your gratitude enhances the value of my friendship too highly; you are the daughter of my particular friend, and I can never feel greater pleasure, than in paying a tribute to her memory, by doing you every service in my power. Charles, time passes swiftly, what tree do you begin with?

CHARLES.

I have finished my account of the principal trees used for heavy timber; the peculiar uses of the light sorts of wood remain for me to mention. Lime is used chiefly in carving, and for such purposes as pill-boxes, &c. The twigs are made into baskets and cradles, and all kinds of wicker-work. The inner bark has been used instead of paper. A copy of one of Cicero's works, written on this bark, was preserved as a great curiosity in Cardinal Mazarine's library.

HENRY.

I have been often greatly amused by watching the basket-maker that lives in the village; he uses osiers as well as the twigs of the lime. The vast variety of things that he makes, with such simple materials, has surprised me; sometimes I have sat down and worked with him; and were I to become very poor, I think I could easily follow his trade.

AUGUSTA.

Pray what variety of things does he make? I cannot recollect any thing but baskets.

HENRY.

In the first place, baskets of various forms and sizes, flaskets, hampers, cages, lattices, cradles, hurdles, wiers for fish, and many other things that I cannot remember. Hazel is the best for hurdles, fishing-rods, and springs to catch birds with.

CECILIA.

Are not osiers a species of willow?

CHARLES.

Yes, they are a kind of low willow found by the water-side; the wood of the willow, of late years, is come into great demand for the purpose of making ladies' hats. It is cut into thin narrow slips, by means of a machine, and woven into the form of a hat, which has a pretty effect. This kind of wood is suited to purposes that require elasticity; the elder, on the contrary, is adapted to uses that need toughness, such as butcher's skewers, &c. Almost every part of this tree has its medicinal use, and pleasant-flavoured wine is made both from the flowers and fruit. Poplar is incomparable for all sorts of white wooden ware, as also for heels of shoes. The hardness of box, and readiness to take a polish, renders it very valuable to the turner for mathematical instruments, pegs, nut-crackers, weaver's shuttles, rulers, rolling-pins, pestles, tops, chessmen, screws, lace bobbins, spoons, combs, &c. Holly affords the whitest wood of any, and is used in making dressing-boxes, and other fancy-works.

Mr. HARCOURT.

Almost innumerable are the uses, to which different parts of trees, growing in every temperature of the world, are applied. The bodies for timber, the bark, leaves, blossoms, fruit, gums, resin, manna, sugar, contribute to our accommodation, and are rendered, by art and ingenuity, subservient to our use. Some trees afford food, others poison; the fibres of some supply us with cloathing, the timber of many with habitations; from some we extract medicines for the use of our maladies; from others, dyes of various hues; some are adapted to form musical instruments by the sonorous quality of their wood; such as maple, fir, yew, and pear-tree; others, deficient in that property, compensate the defect, by excellence of a different kind. Every tree has its peculiar property, and scarce any but may be converted to useful purposes; their branches afford a lodging to birds, their berries supply them with food; numerous insects inhabit every part of them. Let us admire the wise economy of nature, that supports and nourishes one part of her works by the produce of another. The seeds alone of trees and plants feed a vast number of animals, and yet there are a sufficient number left for the purpose of preserving their respective kinds.

Mrs. HARCOURT.

The fecundity of vegetables is equally amazing with that of fishes. Mr. Ray asserts that one thousand and twelve seeds of tobacco weighed only one grain, and that from one tobacco plant, the seed thus calculated amounted to three hundred and sixty thousand. The seeds of the ferns are, by him, supposed to exceed a million on a leaf. This numerous reproduction prevents the accidental extinction of the species, at the same time that it serves for food for the higher order of animation. Nature has provided in a wonderful manner both for the nourishment and preservation of the immature seed. Every seed possesses a reservoir of nutriment, designed for the growth of the future plant; this consists of starch, mucilage, or oil within the coat of the seed; or of sugar, and sub-acid pulp in the fruit, which belong to it. In order to preserve them from injury, some are wrapped in down; as the seeds of the rose, bean, and cotton-plant: others are suspended in a large air-vessel, as those of the bladder-sena, staphylaea, and pea: many are furnished with a sort of wing or feather, as those of the thistle and anemone, which assists their conveyance by the wind from one place to another. There is a great analogy between the seeds of vegetables, and the eggs of animals and insects. They both include a perfect individual of their respective kinds, together with suitable nourishment to bring it to maturity, though the parts are far too minute for our investigation.

AUGUSTA.

Is it possible that so large a tree, as that majestic oak, which we so often admire, could ever be contained in a small acorn?

Mr. HARCOURT.

The fact admits of no doubt; in some plants the embryo is partly visible, by the assistance of the best microscopes; and as nature governs by general laws, it is fair to surmise that the other kinds are propagated in the same manner.

SOPHIA.

Vegetables produce their seeds or embryo young inconsciously, and drop them on the ground, or suffer them to be wafted by the wind where accident directs. Insects shew a higher degree of instinct, and deposit their eggs where they are likely to meet with food suitable to their different natures; and, after providing for their future security, by placing them in a proper situation, die; or, if their short existence is extended beyond one season, leave them to be hatched by the sun, without further care. How superior is the parental solicitude of birds! after composing a habitation for the reception of the eggs, with much labour and ingenuity, with what patience do they confine themselves to the task of hatching them! They seem to have lost every desire for flying about, and sit, day after day, till the young brood is hatched; their cares are then of another kind, they leave the nest for a little while at first, to seek for food, which they distribute equally to their young ones. Their anxiety is continued till the nestlings are capable of providing for themselves, when they seem to forget their past affection, and wholly abandon the objects of their former tenderness to their own management.

Mrs. HARCOURT.

Instinct, or that quality in animals which corresponds with reason in man, is bestowed on each creature in proportion to its rank or order in creation. The gradation of being is something like the links of a mighty chain, the immediate distinctions of which are scarcely perceptible; but when we compare the mineral, vegetable, and animal kingdoms together, the superior excellence, of the latter is obvious; as the lowest degree of animal life is above the highest vegetable production. Let us proceed still further, and make a comparison of the most inferior orders of animals, such as oysters, &c. which seem only to possess a bare existence, void of faculties or enjoyment, with man, a creature endowed with the noble quality of reason, capable of exercising very extensive intellectual powers, and enabled to understand, admire, and investigate the works of his great Creator.

CECILIA.

I never was so sensible of my own dignity before.

Mr. HARCOURT.

Beware, my dear child, of doing any action unworthy of a being of so exalted a rank in the scale of existence; at the same time, learn humility, from the recollection, that it is rational to believe, that there are degrees of intellectual beings, as much above man, as an oyster is below him. We have strangely wandered from our subject. Charles, are you prepared to give us an account of the poison-tree, which you extracted from Dr. Darwin's[*] notes on the Loves of the Plants?

CHARLES.

The upas-tree is situated in the island of Java. It is surrounded on all sides by a circle of high hills and mountains; and the country round it, to the distance of ten or twelve miles from the tree, is entirely barren. Not a tree, or a shrub; nor even the least plant or

---

[*] "The Loves of the Plants" (1789) is Erasmus Darwin's verse exposition of the Linnaean Sexual System of plant classification. Darwin's notes add much additional information. "Loves of the Plants" was issued as Part II of Darwin's *The Botanic Garden* (1791).

grass is to be seen. The destructive effluvia that proceeds from the tree is supposed to be the cause of this steril appearance. The poison which is procured from this tree, is a gum that issues out between the bark and the tree itself, like the camphor. Malefactors, who are sentenced to die for their crimes, are the only persons who collect the poison, and they are allowed this chance of saving their lives. After sentence is pronounced upon them by the judge, they are asked in court, whether they will die by the hands of the executioner, or go to the upas-tree for a box of poison. They commonly prefer the latter proposal, as there is not only some chance of preserving their lives, but also a certainty, in case of their safe return, that a provision will be made for them in future by the emperor. They are also permitted to ask a favour of the emperor, which is generally of a trifling nature, and usually granted. They are then provided with a silver box, in which they are to put the poisonous gum, and are properly instructed how they are to proceed, while they are upon their dangerous expedition. They are told to pay particular attention to the direction of the winds, as they are to go towards the tree before the wind, so that the effluvia from the tree is always blown from them. They are likewise directed to travel with the utmost dispatch, as that is the only method of ensuring a safe return. They are afterwards sent to the house of an old priest, who lives on the nearest habitable spot, appointed by the emperor to reside there, for the purpose of preparing the souls of those criminals for eternity, who are sent to the tree, by prayers and admonitions. To this place they are commonly attended by their friends and relations. When the hour of their departure arrives, the priest puts them on a long leathern cap, with two glasses before their eyes, which comes down as low as their breast, and also provides them with a pair of leathern gloves. Thus equipped, they are conducted by the priest and their relations, about two miles on their journey. Here the priest repeats his instructions, and tells them where they are to look for the tree. He shews them a hill, which they are to ascend, and that on the other side, they will find a rivulet, which will guide them to the upas. They now take leave of each other, and, amidst prayers for their success, the delinquents hasten away. Notwithstanding the precautions that are taken, there are scarcely two out of twenty that escape. It is certain that from fifteen to eighteen miles round this tree, not only no human creature can exist, but that, in that space of ground, no living animal of any kind has ever been discovered. Every man of quality has his dagger or other arms poisoned with the gum of this destructive tree; and in times of war, the Malayans

125

poison the springs, and other waters with it; by this treacherous practice the Dutch suffered greatly during the last war, as it occasioned the loss of half their army. For this reason, they have ever since kept fish in those springs of which they drink, and sentinels are placed near them, who inspect the waters every hour, to see whether the fish are alive. If they march into an enemy's country, they always carry live fish with them, which they throw into the water, some hours before they venture to drink of it, by which means they have been able in some degree to provide for their security.

SOPHIA.

This is a very extraordinary account. How happy is it for mankind that these baneful trees are not commonly found: so subtle and irresistible does their poisonous influence seem to be, that were they scattered in different places, they might destroy all animals and vegetables, and change this beautiful world into a barren waste.

Mrs. HARCOURT.

The most useful and beneficial things are bestowed in greatest plenty, which is an instance of the Divine Goodness, that calls for our daily gratitude.

AUGUSTA.

Of what use can the upas-tree be; would it not have been better, if such trees had never been created?

Mrs. HARCOURT.

The wisdom of the Almighty, in the order of the creation, and our limited capacity to judge of the good of the whole, is a sufficient reply to such questions. But perhaps such instruments of destruction are permitted to make us sensible of our happy situation, and the many blessings we enjoy; at the same time, they serve as monuments of that power that can destroy a guilty world by a variety of means, and may have some influence to restrain the vices of those who are principally affected by sensible objects. The Caoutchouc, or Indian rubber, being the produce of a tree, some account of the manner of its preparation will not be foreign to the present subject. Cecilia will be kind enough to tell us something concerning it.

CECILIA.

It consists of a very elastic resin, produced by a tree, which grows on the banks of the river of the Amazons. It grows to a very great height, perfectly straight, having no branches except at top. Its leaves bear some resemblance to those of the manioc: they are green on the upper part, and white beneath. The seeds are three in number, and contained in a pod, consisting of three cells, not unlike those of the palma christi; and in each of them there is a kernel, which being stripped and boiled in water, yields a thick oil or fat, which the natives use for the same purposes that we do butter. The juice, which is applied to many different uses, is collected chiefly in time of rain, because it flows then most abundantly. They make an incision through the bark, and there issues from it a milky liquor. It is said, that the means employed to harden it, is kept a profound secret. Though some assert, that it thickens, and becomes gradually solid by being exposed to the air. As it becomes solid, it shews an extraordinary degree of flexibility and elasticity. The Indians make boots of it, which water cannot penetrate: they have a method of smoking them, that makes them look like real leather. Bottles are also made of this substance, to the necks of which are fastened hollow reeds, so that the liquor that is contained in them may be squirted through the reeds by pressing the bottle. One of these, filled with water, is always presented to each of their guests at their entertainments, who never fail to make use of it before eating.

HENRY.

How I should laugh to see a company of people squirting water at each other!

Mrs. HARCOURT.

There are various customs in different countries, that appear strange and unaccountable to the eye of an unprejudiced stranger, and seem to have arisen from caprice or accident. Habit renders us insensible to the absurdity of those we see constantly practised. Is it not as reasonable to wish health and happiness to our friends, at every mouthful we eat, as at every glass we drink?

HENRY.

It might be quite as reasonable, but it would appear very comical.

Mrs. HARCOURT.

Civility requires that a traveller should comply with the customs of the countries through which he passes, provided they be perfectly harmless and innocent. Cecilia, continue your account of the caoutchouc.

CECILIA.

Flambeaux made of this resin give a brilliant light, and have no bad smell. A kind of cloth is also prepared from it, which the inhabitants of Quito apply to the same purposes as our oil-cloth, or sail-cloth. It is also formed into a variety of figures by means of earthen moulds, that serve both for use and ornament.

Mr. HARCOURT.

Ever since this resin has been known in Europe, its chemical qualities, and other interesting properties, have been very diligently investigated. Its solidity, flexibility and elasticity, added to its quality of resisting the action of aqueous, spirituous, saline, oily, and other common solvents, render it extremely fit for the construction of tubes and other instruments, in which these properties are wanted. You have all experienced its usefulness in drawing, by erasing the erroneous strokes of black lead pencils, which has occasioned many to call it, Lead-eater. Were we acquainted with the different properties of all the forest-trees, that grow in the various climates of the earth, the subject would be almost inexhaustible, and would furnish us with new matter of admiration of the power and wisdom that formed them, and endued each with its peculiar distinction. Of those that are known, we have only mentioned the most obvious and striking, and such as we are familiar with by name, from using their productions. Children, recollect whether you cannot enrich our list, by adding an account of any trees remarkable for their produce or beauty, which Charles has forgotten or omitted.

SOPHIA.

The nutmeg-tree is found in the East-Indies, and is said to resemble a pear-tree; the fruit is inclosed in four covers; a thick fleshy coat, something like that of the walnut, contains the whole, which opens of itself when ripe: under this lies a thin reddish kind of net-work, of an agreeable smell and aromatic taste, which we call mace, and is as valuable as the fruit itself; the shell is the third covering, and is hard, thin, and blackish; under this is a greenish film, of no use, and in it is found the nutmeg. According to Tavernier, birds are the instruments of propagating these trees by eating the nutmegs, and afterwards dropping them undigested upon the ground, and being softened and prepared for growth by the heat of the stomach, they readily take root. These birds are not permitted to be killed, on account of this circumstance, as the productions of this tree afford a very lucrative branch of commerce to the Dutch East-India Company, who monopolize the spice-trade, and by that means render it very profitable. Nutmegs and mace give an elegant flavour to high-seasoned dishes, and are frequently used in medicine.

AUGUSTA.

I have seen and used the different kinds of spices, without ever reflecting on their nature; are cinnamon and cloves also the produce of trees?

SOPHIA.

Cinnamon is the bark of a tree, chiefly growing in the island of Ceylon, and cloves are the fruit of a tall tree found in different parts of the East-Indies.

Mrs. HARCOURT.

The tropical climates far excel those that approach nearer the Poles, in the beauty of the feathered race; their colours are more vivid, and dazzle with a richness and brilliancy, that the inhabitants of our groves are not adorned with; but, as if Nature took delight in dividing her gifts, they are deficient in the variety and extent of their tuneful powers, and must yield to the superior music of our warblers. In the vegetable productions, they rise above us also in magnitude, luxuriancy, and fragrance. The groves of pimento-trees in the West-Indies fill the air with their odours; their fruit is a small berry, which we call allspice, because it partakes of the flavour of many of the spices of the East. The pimento refuses the culture of man, and flourishes best when it grows spontaneously. It is a tree of great beauty; the trunk is of a grey colour, smooth and shining; it produces beautiful white flowers, which blow in the months of July and August. The leaves are equally fragrant with the fruit, and yield an odoriferous oil, which, when distilled, frequently passes for oil of cloves.

SOPHIA.

Dr. Hawkesworth relates that the bread-fruit is found at Otaheite, in the South Sea, on a tree about the size of a middling oak. It is as large as our gourds, and the surface covered with a kind of network. The eatable part lies between the skin and the core: it is as white as snow, and of the consistence of new bread. It has an insipid sweetish taste, resembling that of the crumb of wheaten bread, mixed with a Jerusalem artichoke. It is roasted and baked before it is eaten, and admirably supplies the place of bread, to a people ignorant of the arts of cultivation.

CECILIA.

I must not suffer my favourite mulberry-tree to be forgotten; when adorned with the yellow cones of the silk-worm, like so many balls of gold, I think its appearance must equal the beauty of any you have mentioned; and we owe to the insect it nourishes and maintains, the most delicate and agreeable texture that we wear; therefore you must allow it is inferior to few in usefulness.

Mr. HARCOURT.

Cecilia is determined to defend her favourite with spirit; and indeed she has done it ably, for without the mulberry-tree, we must relinquish the use of silk, so well adapted to the clothing the inhabitants of warm climates, and which contributes so much to the elegance and magnificence of dress and furniture, in all countries where it is known; but, my dear children, where time is spent agreeably, it also passes swiftly. Our hour of separation is already past. Let us retire, and seek that repose, which is necessary to refresh our weary spirits, and invigorate us for the pursuits of to-morrow.

CONVERSATION 16

Mr. HARCOURT.

OUR late conversations on the subject of the various kinds of timber have led me to consider their extensive use in the building of ships; whether for the purpose of conveying us to the distant regions of the earth, or transporting the productions of one climate to its opposite extreme.

HENRY.

Pray, tell us how they first contrived to build a ship; it must be very curious to know the manner of putting the parts together on the water.

AUGUSTA.

I am far more desirous of being informed of the name of the man, who had sufficient courage to venture upon so unstable an element.

Mrs. HARCOURT.

A long period of time was necessary to bring either navigation, or the art of constructing vessels, to any degree of perfection. The first efforts were rude and imperfect. Observation taught the early inhabitants of the earth that light substances floated upon the surface of the water; experience, that sure, but slow guide, instructed them, that any thing would swim, that displaced a body of the fluid equal to its own weight. It is probable that the inhabitants of countries bordering on the sea, at first only ventured close along the shore, on a few planks fastened together, and pushed themselves along by the assistance of a stick or pole: repeated attempts suggested various improvements, till by degrees, men became capable of building floating houses, and sailing in them to the most distant regions of the earth. The advancement of science in general, still contributes to improve and perfect the invention of constructing vessels, and guiding them through the pathless ocean. That small instrument, the mariner's compass, said to be the contrivance of Flavio, a Neapolitan, about the beginning of the fourteenth century, has been of the greatest advantage in enabling persons at sea to know the course they are pursuing. It principally consists of a needle of iron, impregnated with the magnetic powers of the load-stone, which influences it always to point nearly to the north: thus, by being exactly acquainted with one of the cardinal points, it is easy to find out the others. As Charles is a better classical scholar than I am, I leave him to reply to Augusta's query.

CHARLES.

It is supposed that Neptune, called by the pagans, god of the sea, was the founder of these inventions, and that his discovery was immortalized by attributing to him the dominion of the element he had subdued. Many give the honour to Daedalus, and imagine that the wings he is said to have invented, to save himself from the resentment of Minos, king of Crete, whom he had offended, were nothing but sails, which he applied to the vessel in which he escaped; but all these accounts are uncertain. Scripture affords us some authentic records. Noah was certainly one of the earliest ship-builders, and the ark the first large vessel that is mentioned in history. Profane history relates an extraordinary account of two other ships of prodigious magnitude; the first built by order of Ptolemy Philopater, king of Egypt, which carried four thousand rowers, four hundred sailors, and three thousand soldiers; the other belonged to Hiero, king of Sicily, and was built under the direction of Archimedes. It contained all the variety of apartments belonging to a palace; banqueting-rooms, galleries, gardens, fishponds, stables, mills, baths, a temple of Venus, &c. and to render it complete, it was encompassed with an iron rampart, and eight towers, with walls and bulwarks, furnished with machines of war.

Mr. HARCOURT.

When the history of a very remote period records events that exceed rational belief, it is reasonable to suppose, that the circumstance related was regarded as extraordinary at the time it happened; and that the historian, desirous of transmitting the fame of his native country to posterity, has enlarged the fact, and related it in the glowing colours of fiction. In this light I consider the description of Hiero's vessel. But to return to the simple inventions of the earliest navigators, the various tribes of savage nations, that inhabit the sea-coast, will throw the best light on the subject. Canoe is the name given to the little boats generally used by those who dwell in both Indies, as well as by the negroes in Guinea. They generally make them of the trunks of trees hollowed out, and sometimes of pieces of bark fastened together: they differ in size, according to the tree of which they are made; they are rowed with paddles, something like the oars of a boat, and but rarely carry sails. The loading is placed at the bottom; but, as they have no ballast, they are frequently turned upside down. The want of a rudder, with which they are not furnished, is supplied by the hind paddles. The negroes of Guinea used the same sort of canoe, though made in a different manner: they are long shaped, having only room for one person in width, and seven or eight in length, and shew but little of the wood above the water. Those accustomed to row them are extremely dexterous, not only in striking the paddles with cadence and uniformity, by which the canoes seem to skim along the surface of the water; but also in balancing the vessel with their bodies, and preventing their overturning, which, without this address, must continually happen from their extreme lightness; but what is still more extraordinary, that when this accident does occur, many of them have the dexterity to turn them up again even in the water, and remount them.

CECILIA.

I have often remarked, that savages shew great ingenuity in their simple contrivances, and that they excel the inhabitants of civilized countries in personal address and dexterity. What European can vie with some of the Indians in running, when they pursue their game in hunting? or in patience, whilst they suffer the want of food, when they happen to be disappointed of obtaining it in the woods? The art with which they contrive stratagems in war, to deceive their enemies, shews great cunning and skill; though I despise the principle, I admire the fertility of their invention. When I reflect upon their superiority in these things, I am discontented, because I cannot find a satisfactory reason why ignorance should excel knowledge in any thing.

Mr. HARCOURT.

There are many causes why a savage should perform acts of skill and dexterity, in a manner superior to a person, whose mind has been enriched by the cultivation of science; but there can exist no instance of ignorance being preferable to knowledge. The intellectual powers of a savage, though capable of receiving the same impressions, as a man of science, are, from want of education, confined to very few objects; on those he bestows his whole attention, and consequently attains a great degree of perfection in the things that belong to them. Do you not think that Charles would jump better than any of his acquaintance, if he passed whole days or weeks in no other occupation but that exercise?

CECILIA.

Certainly; I have no doubt of it.

SOPHIA.

The subsistence of savages depends so much upon their success in fishing and hunting, that, without skill in these arts, they must frequently be destitute of provisions; it is likely, therefore, that their whole education consists in attaining this dexterity. Although they manage their canoes with such surprising cleverness, I suppose they do not venture far out to sea.

Mr. HARCOURT.

Seldom to a greater distance from shore than four leagues. They weave mats with rushes, of which they make the sails. On return from a voyage, the canoes are not left in the water, but drawn on shore, and suspended by the two ends, till they are dry, in which state they are so light, that two men can easily carry them on their shoulders. Different causes have operated in forming the peculiar character of different nations. The narrowness and poverty of the land inhabited by the Phoenicians and Tyrians, combining with their natural genius for traffic, rendered them the first nation of navigators among the ancients. Lebanon and the other neighbouring mountains supplying them with excellent wood for ship building, they were in possession of a numerous fleet, before other nations had acquired any knowledge in the art beyond that of coasting in small vessels. The commerce they established with foreign countries, by the means of their skill in naval affairs, enriched them to an extraordinary pitch of opulence. The employment given to such numbers of hands, by this enterprising and commercial spirit, increased the population of the country to such a degree, that they were obliged to found colonies in other countries, the principal of which was that of Carthage. In time, Carthage became more powerful than the mother country, and extended her navigation into Europe, as far north as Britain. The rivalship that subsisted between the states of Carthage and Rome, for many years, ended in the total destruction of the former, and left Rome without a competitor. This celebrated city in her turn became the prey of the Goths and Vandals, and with her fell, not only learning and the polite arts, but also the useful one of navigation declined rather than advanced for some time. The Crusades, that monument of human folly and enthusiasm, contributed to restore and accelerate the revival of commerce and navigation, by the number of vessels that were necessary to convey those vast armies into Asia, on this wild enterprise. The invention of the compass, combined with the voyages of discovery and other causes, to promote the advancement of this useful branch of science, and raise it to its present state.

CHARLES.

Which of the nations of Europe patronised the early voyages of discovery?

Mr. HARCOURT.

Had John II of Portugal listened to the proposal of Columbus, who was a native of Genoa, to give him encouragement to explore a passage to India, by sailing towards the west, across the Atlantic Ocean, that nation might have claimed this honour; but John treated his scheme with contempt; and Columbus, disgusted with his behaviour, quitted Portugal, and went to Spain, in order to apply to Ferdinand and Isabella, who reigned conjointly at that time. Eight years were spent in repeated applications before he succeeded. At length, in August 1492, this great man, furnished with a small fleet of three ships, set sail, and steered directly for the Canary Islands; from thence he proceeded due west, through unfrequented and unknown seas; and after many difficulties, arrived at Guanharic, one of the large cluster of islands, called the Bahama Isles, and returned to Spain, without having obtained his principal object, of discovering another continent, which he supposed to exist on the western side of the globe. He made a second voyage without any better success. Undaunted by so many disappointments, he undertook a third voyage, and actually fell in with the vast continent of America; which, after all his indefatigable labour, received its name from a Florentine, Americus Vesputius, who only followed the footsteps he had marked out. Succeeding navigators made new discoveries, and Portugal at length saw the advantages of patronising these enterprises. It does not seem that our countrymen turned their attention this way till a later period. In 1577, Sir Francis Drake undertook and completed a voyage round the world, in about three years. Our late discoveries have been principally in the Pacific Ocean, and, to the honour of the

British nation, the name of Captain Cook will ever remain distinguished among the chief navigators. It was not the thirst of digging the gold from the mine, but the desire of diffusing the arts and advantages of civilization among his fellow creatures, that induced him to explore unknown seas. He wandered from one nation of strangers to another, offering the olive branch of peace, and desired rather to form an alliance of friendship with them, than to oppress them by tyranny and injustice.

CHARLES.

Although England is now celebrated for the superiority of her navy, it appears that the northern parts of the world were slow in attaining this perfection; for, when Caesar invaded Britain, the natives opposed him in vessels of an odd form, like large tubs, the sails were composed of leather, and iron chains supplied the place of cables.

Mrs. HARCOURT.

The Saxons, after being some time settled in this island, became sensible that its surest defence would be a formidable navy, and applied themselves vigorously to build ships of war. Ethelred, in order to maintain a powerful force at sea, made a law, that whoever possessed 300 hides* of land, should build and man one ship for the defence of his country. Our insular situation has obliged us to bestow great attention in improving and advancing the art of ship-building to perfection. It is also our best policy to encourage a nursery of British seamen, which is done in part by the numbers that are employed in the Newcastle colliers, and other trade fleets. This is the reason that coal-pits in the neighbourhood of London are not suffered to be worked. The superiority of the British fleet for strength and beauty, as well as for the bravery of its mariners, is indisputed, and our nation has long been considered as mistress of the sea.

---

* A hide of land was formerly reckoned 100 acres. [P.W.]

SOPHIA.

In the reign of Queen Elizabeth our royal navy was in a very flourishing condition.

Mr. HARCOURT.

The progress of commerce and navigation naturally keep pace together. Trade first gave occasion to the fitting out large fleets of ships, and as that increased, the cargoes became more valuable, and each nation, jealous of her property, found ships of war necessary to convoy her merchantmen in safety to their destined ports. Ships, intended for different purposes, required a variety of forms and sizes, as well as a diversity of construction and rigging. The form of fishes being admirably adapted to divide the fluid element, and make a way through the waters, furnished hints to ship-builders in forming the hulks of vessels. Naval architecture comprehends three principal objects. In the first place, it is necessary to give the ship such an exterior form, as may be best suited to the service for which she is designed. Secondly, to find the proper figures of all the pieces of timber that compose a ship. And lastly, to provide suitable accommodations for the officers and crew, as well as for the cargo, furniture, provisions, artillery, and ammunition. A ship of war should be able to sail swiftly, and carry her lower tier of guns properly; it is necessary for a merchant-ship to contain a large cargo of goods, and be navigated with few hands; and each kind should be able to carry sail firmly, steer well, drive little to leeward, and sustain the shocks of the sea without being much strained. Charles you have visited a dock-yard, can you give your brother a satisfactory account of the method used in building ships?

CHARLES.

The vessels, that I saw building, were supported in the dock, or upon a wharf, by a number of solid blocks of timber, placed parallel, and at equal distances from each other. The workmen call this being on the stocks.

Mr. HARCOURT.

This is an answer to your enquiry, Henry, how they contrived to build ships upon the water: had you reflected a moment, you would not have asked such a silly question.

HENRY.

I asked without considering that it would be impossible. Forgive me, if I am now desirous of knowing how such large bodies are removed into the water.

Mrs. HARCOURT.

I commend a proper curiosity; but, in future, before you ask a question, consider whether it be a reasonable one, and whether, by reflection on the subject, you cannot resolve it yourself. When they begin to build a ship, it is supported upon strong platforms, inclined towards the water. All things being ready for the launch, the wedges and supporters are cut away, and the parts over which the vessel is to pass, are well daubed with grease and soap, to make her slide more easily. Every obstruction being removed, by degrees she slides into the water. Very large vessels are frequently built in dry docks, and when finished, the flood-gates of the dock-yard are opened, and the water rushes in, and raises the vessel to the surface. Charles, are you able to recollect the principal parts that compose a ship? I took some pains to make you master of the subject.

CHARLES.

It is a difficult one, but I will endeavour to give the company the clearest idea of them in my power. The first piece of timber laid upon the block is generally the keel; the pieces of the keel are scarped together, a term used for fastening large pieces of timber together in a manner somewhat similar to what the carpenters call dove-tail; thus united, they form one entire piece, which constitutes the length of the vessel below. At one extremity of the keel is erected the stem, which is a circular piece of timber, into which her two sides are fixed at the fore end: at the other extremity of the keel, is elevated the stern-post, into which are fastened the after-planks, and in the stern-post hangs the rudder. The transoms and fashion pieces are large pieces of timber that form the width of the ship. These being strongly united into one frame, are elevated upon the stern-post, and the whole forms the structure of the stern, upon which the galleries and windows, with their ornaments, are afterwards built. The stern and stern-post being thus elevated upon the keel, and the keel being raised at its two extremities by pieces of wood, the midship floor timber is placed across the keel. The floor timbers, both before and abaft* the midship frame is then stationed in its proper place upon the keel; after which the kelson, which is, the next piece of timber to the keel, and lying directly over it, is fixed across the middle of the floor timber. The futtocks, or ribs, which form the sides, are then raised upon the floor timbers, and the top timbers being afterwards fastened to the head of the futtocks, completes the exterior figure of the whole.

Mr. HARCOURT.

Considering the subject is so intricate, you have described it with tolerable clearness.

Mrs. HARCOURT.

You have given us an idea of the external figure of a ship, the inside finishing also requires a great deal of art. It is divided into several decks or floors, destined to different uses. Large ships have three decks, smaller but two, and there are vessels that are only half decked. The decks are divided into several apartments. The best cabin, for there are sometimes more than one, corresponds with the drawing-room of a house, and is appropriated to the reception of visiters. The cuddy serves for an eating-parlour; there is also on board an Indiaman a cabin, behind the cuddy, called the round-house. Besides these, separate apartments are provided for the different officers, as cook-room, gun-room, &c. &c.

HENRY.

Do they lie in such beds as we do?

Mrs. HARCOURT.

They would find them very inconvenient, on account of the motion of the ship; they use hammocks at sea, which are beds hung to the ceiling, and they swing backwards and forwards as the ship rolls.

---

* Abaft, a sea term for behind. [P.W.]

Mr. HARCOURT.

A ship is very imperfectly described without naming the masts, sails, and rigging. The masts are very tall poles fixed in the deck, to which are attached the sails and the rigging. The sails are generally made of a peculiar kind of coarse hempen cloth, and their use is to gather the wind, by the force of which the vessel is driven along; the rigging is composed of ropes, and serves to furl and unfurl the sails as occasion requires; it also forms a sort of rope-ladders, by which the expert mariners ascend to the top of the mast.

CECILIA.

It must require a vast sum of money to build a ship.

Mr. HARCOURT.

A man of war of 74 guns is calculated to cost £30,000, before she is armed or equipped.

CHARLES.

What an immense sum must be requisite to raise and maintain a fleet! Into how many orders or ranks is the British fleet divided?

Mrs. HARCOURT.

It is distributed into six rates, exclusive of the inferior vessels that usually attend on naval armaments; as sloops of war, armed ships, bomb-ketches, fire-ships, &c. Ships of the first rate mount an hundred cannon, they are manned with 850 men, including officers, seamen, marines, and servants. A captain of a man of war, when on board, is an absolute sovereign, and rules with unlimited sway, but on his return is liable to give account of his conduct in a court martial, as it is a principal of the British constitution, that every subject, of whatever rank, if injured at sea or land, has an equal right to redress.

AUGUSTA.

Pray what difference is there in the meaning of the words ship and vessel?

Mr. HARCOURT.

Vessel comprehends all floating machines, that move in water; we distinguish them into two general classes; high-bottomed, or

140

decked vessels, which are those that move wholly with wind and sail, and live in all seas; and flat-bottomed vessels, which go both by oars and sails, such as boats, barges, wherries, etc.

HENRY.

You mentioned a rudder just now, I do not know what it is.

Mr. HARCOURT.

The rudder is a piece of timber suspended to the stern-post, by which the vessel is guided, in this or that direction, according as the sides of the rudder are opposed to the water. An anchor is a large strong piece of iron, crooked at one end, and formed into two barbs, resembling a double hook, and fastened at the other end by a cable; its use is to keep the vessel confined to one place, by letting it down into the ground.

Mrs. HARCOURT.

As it is sometimes their last resource in time of danger, it is considered as emblematical of hope, which is frequently represented by a female figure, resting upon an anchor, and looking up to Heaven for deliverance.

SOPHIA.

Are not flags displayed on the masts of ships, to denote to what nation they belong?

Mr. HARCOURT.

They not only serve that purpose, but also distinguish the rank of the admiral or commander on board. In the British navy the flags are either red, white, or blue. The admiral or commander in chief carries his flag on the foremast, and that of the rear admiral is carried on the mizen-mast. Different signals are used at sea, according to circumstances; and, during an engagement, the orders of a commander are given and understood with wonderful precision. James II is said to have invented the principal signals used in our fleet.

CECILIA.

I cannot imagine how the poor sailors avoid running against the rocks in a dark night.

SOPHIA.

Light-houses are erected in proper situations, to warn them of their danger, where such large fires are made as to be visible at a considerable distance. The Pharos of Alexandria was a building of this kind. It was esteemed one of the seven wonders of the world, on account of the beauty of its structure, and the richness of its materials. It stood on a small island at the mouth of the Nile, and consisted of several stones raised one over another, adorned with columns, ballustrades, and galleries of the finest marble and workmanship, to which account some writers add, that the architect contrived to fix mirrors so artificially against the highest galleries, that all the vessels, that sailed on the sea for a considerable distance, were reflected in them.

Mrs. HARCOURT.

The clock strikes, and warns us that it is time to retire. Henry has been so attentive, that I expect he will dream of undertaking a voyage.

HENRY.

I wish I may, by that means I should enjoy the pleasure without partaking of the danger.

Mrs. HARCOURT.

Good night, my little, sleepy sailor. Adieu, dear children.

CONVERSATION 17

HENRY.

I HAVE longed all the day for the time of meeting. I have been thinking of several things concerning ships, which appear wonderful to me: in the first place, I cannot imagine how they contrive to store up provisions for so many people for several months without spoiling; we are obliged to go to market almost every day, but you know there are no shops at sea.

Mrs. HARCOURT.

Consequently the ship's crew cannot live on fresh meat, neither can they procure fresh vegetables, which, with the want of fresh water, are the principal causes of that dreadful disease, called the sea scurvy, to which persons in long voyages are very subject. Beef and pork, well salted down, with hard biscuit, form the usual food of a sailor.

AUGUSTA.

I cannot eat either salt meat or hard biscuit; what would become of me, were I obliged to go to a very distant country?

SOPHIA.

Necessity, my dear Augusta, has taught many to submit to great hardships; suppose your father were obliged to go to the West-Indies, would you prefer being separated from him, or attending him thither, and suffering from some inconveniencies for a few weeks; surely you would not hesitate which to chuse?

AUGUSTA.

My father frequently tells me, that it is not unlikely that his affairs will require his presence in Jamaica. I have entreated him to let me go with him, but I never considered the difficulties of the voyage. Accustomed as I have been to a variety of dishes every day at table, and a dessert of fruit and preserves afterwards, I should find it hard fare to dine on salt beef and biscuit, and to exchange my soft bed for a hammock.

Mr. HARCOURT.

This confession shews the great inconvenience of an habitual indulgence in our mode of living; had you been used to eat only of one dish, and sleep upon a mattress, you might easily have accommodated yourself to an alteration for the worse for a little time. Temperance is not only a virtue, but a great advantage to health, and on many occasions diminishes the difficulties we are liable to meet with. One reflection ought to be sufficient to reconcile us to any temporary hardship, that thousands of our fellow creatures suffer daily, what we think so painful to undergo for a few hours. The consideration of these things will teach us to transfer a little of that solicitude for our own personal enjoyment, to a tender care for the wants and suffering of others.

CHARLES.

The captains and officers have their tables supplied with fresh provisions; sheep, pigs and poultry are kept on board ships for that purpose. I have also seen a cow which afforded milk and cream for the captain's table. Minced meat and sweet-meats are generally among his stores, and any other delicacy that will keep; therefore, Augusta, you may lay aside your apprehensions, for although you could not enjoy all the luxuries you do at home, you may make a tolerable shift for a month or two.

CECILIA.

The comparison of my condition, and that of the poor sailors, would prevent my enjoyment of the indulgences that my superior rank procured me.

Mrs. HARCOURT.

Bring that principal home to your own heart; you constantly enjoy many gratifications, that our poor neighbour Mary Benson has not even an idea of.

CECILIA.

That very thought reconciles me to the difference; but were she a spectator of my daily meals, and obliged to rest contented with her present scanty fare, I should be induced to go shares with her.

144

Mr. HARCOURT.

Our wants vary according to our habits and education; let us be careful not to increase them by pampering a false taste for unnecessary indulgence; a life of hardship is not confined to sailors, many employments subject those, who are engaged in them, to endure it patiently. Miners are deprived of light, and the society of the rest of mankind. Those who work in the quicksilver mines are said not only to lose their health, but generally die in a few years; extremes of heat and cold, hard labour, and scanty fare are the portion of the greater part of mankind; but happiness does not depend upon the enjoyment of luxury; these people possess as large a share of it as their richer and envied neighbours; each condition has its advantage; we are the children of one common parent, who has deemed it wise to distribute mankind into different ranks and orders in society, and to render the poor and the rich dependent on each other, that they may be united by the powerful tie of reciprocal benevolence and affection.

SOPHIA.

I believe I should suffer most from want of fresh water; what a contrivance do they use as a substitute for this necessary comfort?

Mr. HARCOURT.

Many ingenious philosophers have bestowed much time and attention to remedy this defect; the simplest and best method of distilling sea-water, and rendering it fresh, is the invention of Dr. Irving. In order to have a clear idea of his method of accomplishing this desirable purpose; suppose a tea-kettle to be made without a spout, and a hole in the lid in the place of the knob; let this kettle be filled with sea-water, the fresh vapour, which arises from the sea-water, as it boils, will issue through the hole in the lid; fix the mouth of a tube in that hole, and the vapour of fresh water will pass through the tube, and may be collected by fitting a proper vessel to receive it to the end of the tube. Dr. Irving, in a similar manner, has adapted a tin, iron, or copper tube, of suitable dimensions, to the lid of the common kettle, used for boiling the provisions on board a ship. The fresh vapour, which arises from boiling sea-water in the kettle, passes through this tube into a hogshead, which serves as a reservoir.

CHARLES.

This is ingenious, and may alleviate the evil in a degree; but I cannot suppose it can be so agreeable as clear fresh water from a spring, and it must be scarcely possible to procure a sufficient quantity for the comfortable accommodation of so many persons.

Mrs. HARCOURT.

Fresh water is often far more precious than the richest wines on board a ship; the poor men have frequently been obliged to be limited to a certain quantity of it a day. True riches consist in a sufficiency of those things that are necessary to our life and health. Of what use would gold be to a man in a desert? a cup of cold water, or a sack of corn would be, in comparison, an inestimable treasure.

CECILIA.

Surely it must be difficult to preserve the health of persons confined long on board, especially in warm climates.

Mr. HARCOURT.

A considerate humane commander pays great attention to the health and morals of his ship's company; cleanliness, and the free admission of fresh air between decks, are points of the utmost importance, as well as a sufficient supply of such vegetable food as can be preserved; as peas, oatmeal, etc. After every precaution that can be taken, there are inconveniences peculiar to this manner of life.

HENRY.

The desire of seeing foreign countries, with the different manners and customs of the inhabitants, would influence me to face every danger and overcome every difficulty.

Mr. HARCOURT.

Henry is quite a hero; many have felt an invincible inclination for going to sea, which cannot be accounted for, on any other principles, than that men are formed with various propensities, adapting them to a variety of pursuits. Were it otherwise, all men would chuse the easiest profession, and no one would be found to undertake any employment, that threatened either difficulty or danger.

146

AUGUSTA.

In relating the progress of navigation, crusades were mentioned; I should be glad to be informed what they were, as I am entirely ignorant of the meaning of the word.

Mrs. HARCOURT.

Towards the end of the eleventh century, the zeal of a fanatical monk, called Peter the Hermit, who conceived the idea of leading all the forces of Christendom against the infidels, and of driving them out of the possession of the Holy-Land, was sufficient to give a beginning to this wild undertaking. He ran from province to province with a crucifix in his hand, exciting princes and people to this holy war. Wherever he came, they caught the infection of his enthusiasm, not only nobles and warriors, but men in the more humble stations of life: shepherds left their flocks, and mechanics their occupations; nay, even women and children engaged with ardour in this enterprise, which was esteemed sacred and meritorious; contemporary authors assert, that six millions of persons assumed the cross, which was the badge that distinguished such as devoted themselves to this holy warfare. But from these expeditions, extravagant as they were, beneficial consequences arose, which had neither been foreseen nor intended. It was not possible for the crusaders to travel through so many countries without receiving information and improvement, which they communicated to their respective countries, at their return. The necessary provision and accommodation for such vast numbers of people excited a spirit of commerce, and in its consequences advanced the progress of navigation; a spirit of improvement is raised by the communication of different nations; those people, who are destitute of commerce, remain a long time stationary.

SOPHIA.

How often do we see good arise out of apparent evil? Who could have supposed that the mistaken enthusiasm of an obscure monk could have been productive of such public benefit?

Mr. HARCOURT.

It is useful to trace things to their causes; many events that have made great noise in the world, have arisen from causes apparently trifling, and inadequate to the effects produced. The means of introducing the reformation into this country, with all its happy consequences, was the unlawful love of Henry VIII for Anne Boleyn. He sought only his own gratification; but the hand of Providence converted his corrupt inclinations into an instrument of good to his people. Discoveries in the arts have frequently been the result of accident. This should teach us the habit of observation. The bulk of mankind observe little, and reflect less, which accounts for many persons in advanced life having few ideas of their own.

CECILIA.

You have so often inculcated the advantage of observing the nature and texture of every thing we use, that it is become an amusing custom, when we are by ourselves, to question each other on the qualities of those things that attract our notice. This morning at breakfast, tea, coffee, and chocolate were the subjects of enquiry; none of us were capable of giving a good account of them, without having recourse to books for information; we each chose our topic, and I believe Henry can inform us in what manner coffee is cultivated and prepared. Charles selected the cacao-tree for his investigation. The tea-tree of course fell to my share.

Mrs. HARCOURT.

Pray let us be amused with the result of your researches. Cecilia, your brothers will not take the lead, they resign the precedence to you.

CECILIA.

The tea-tree, according to Linnaeus, is of the polyandria monogynia class; the cup is a very small, plane, permanent perianthium, divided into five or six roundish obtuse leaves; the flower consists of six or nine large roundish, concave, and equal petals; the stamina are numerous filaments, about two hundred, and are very slender, capillary, and shorter than the flower; the antherae are simple; the germin of the pestil is globose and trigonal; the style is subulated, and of the length of the stamina; the stigma is simple; the fruit is a capsule, formed of three globular bodies growing together; it contains three cells, and opens into three parts at the top. The seeds are single, globose, and internally annulated. It is supposed that there is but one species of this tree, and that the difference between green and bohea tea, consists only in the manner of cultivation, and drying the leaves. The root resembles that of the peach-tree, the leaves are long and narrow, and jagged all round. The flower is much like that of the wild rose, but smaller; the fruit contains two or three seeds of a mouse colour, including each a kernel. These are the seeds by which the plant is propagated; several of these are put promiscuously into a hole, four or five inches deep, at proper distances from each other, and require no other care. In about seven years, the shrub rises to a man's height, which it seldom greatly exceeds.

Mr. HARCOURT.

You have forgotten to tell us of what country this shrub is native.

CECILIA.

It is cultivated in Japan, and grows abundantly in China, where whole fields are planted with it, as it forms a very extensive article of commerce among the Chinese. It loves to grow in valleys, at the foot of mountains, and upon the banks of rivers, where it enjoys a southern exposure to the sun, though it endures considerable variations of heat and cold flourishing through the different degrees of climate in the extensive kingdom of China. Sometimes the tea-trees grow on the steep declivities of hills, when it is dangerous, and in some cases impracticable to get at them. The Chinese are said to make use of the large monkeys, that dwell among these cliffs, to assist them in obtaining the valuable leaves of the tea-trees: they irritate these animals, and, in revenge, they climb trees, and break off branches, and throw them down the precipice, which give the gatherers an opportunity of reaching them.

AUGUSTA.

What part of this shrub is applied to our use?

CECILIA.

The leaves constitute the tea we use; the best time to gather them is whilst they are small, young, and juicy; they are plucked carefully one by one; and, notwithstanding the tediousness of this operation, the labourers are able to gather from four to fifteen pounds each, in one day. The buildings, or drying houses, that are erected for curing tea, contain from five to twenty small furnaces, each having at the top a large flat iron pan. There is also a long low table, covered with mats, on which the leaves are laid, and rolled by workmen, who sit round it; the iron pan being heated, to a certain degree, by a little fire made in the furnace underneath, a

149

few pounds of the fresh gathered leaves are put upon the pan, the fresh and juicy leaves crack when they touch the pan, and it is the business of the operator to shift them as quick as possible with his bare hands, till they become too hot to be endured. At this instant he takes off the leaves with a kind of a shovel, and pours them on the mats before the rollers, who, taking small quantities at a time, roll them in the palms of their hands in one direction, while others are fanning them, that they may cool the more speedily, and retain their curl the longer. This process is repeated two or three times, or oftener, before the tea is put into the stores, in order that all the moisture of the leaves may be thoroughly dissipated, and their curl more completely preserved. On every repetition the pan is less heated, and the operation performed more slowly and cautiously; the tea is then separated into the different kinds, and deposited in the store for domestic use or exportation. The Chinese drink tea more frequently than the Europeans; it is the chief treat, with which they regale their friends; and it is said, that it is a branch of polite education in that country, to learn to infuse and serve it gracefully. It was introduced into Europe, very early in the last century by the Dutch East-India Company. About the year 1666, a quantity of it was imported from Holland, by Lord Arlington, and Lord Ossory, at which time it was sold for sixty shillings a pound. The present consumption of it is immense, nineteen millions of pounds being annually imported since the commutation act took place.

SOPHIA.

I think this agreeable beverage is reckoned unwholesome.

CECILIA.

The faculty reckon it very much so, to some constitutions, particularly low nervous habits; at the same time, they allow that the same quantity of warm water might be nearly as prejudicial; therefore I am willing to drink it cool, provided I may be permitted to enjoy this enlivening repast, which always seems superior in sociability and cheerfulness to every other meal in the day.

Mr. HARCOURT.

At the same time that you mention its pernicious qualities, it is but fair to remark, that it is in some cases valued as a medicine, and is acknowledged to be the most powerful restorative to the spirits after fatigue of body or mind.

Mrs. HARCOURT.

The general use of it among the poor and laborious part of mankind, I consider baneful to them in many respects; it consumes a large part of their scanty earnings, that might be expended in more nutritious food, and though it gives a temporary animation to their wearied spirits, it is not capable of renewing their strength, exhausted by the fatigues of the day; the same money laid out in milk would be more beneficial and nourishing to themselves and their infants; not that I would wholly deprive them of this solace, but I believe it would redound to their advantage, if it were only used occasionally by the way of treat.

CECILIA.

I have no addition to make to my account; therefore I hope Charles is ready to begin.

CHARLES.

The cacao, or chocolate-nut, is a native of South-America, and is said to have been originally conveyed to Hispaniola from some of the provinces of New Spain, where it was not only used as an article of nourishment by the natives, but likewise served the purpose of money, being employed as a medium in barter; one hundred and fifty of the nuts were considered as nearly equivalent to a ryal by the Spaniards. It is a genus of the polyadelphia pentandria class; the flower has five petals, and five erect stamina; in the centre is placed the oval germin, which afterwards becomes an oblong pod, ending in a point, which is divided into five cells, filled with oval, compressed, fleshy seeds. The cacao-tree, both in size and shape, has some resemblance to a young black-heart cherry-tree. The flower is of a saffron-colour, extremely beautiful, and the pods, which, when green, are much like a cucumber, proceed immediately from all part of the body and larger branches. Each pod may contain from twenty to thirty nuts or kernels, not unlike almonds. These nuts are first dried in the sun, and then packed for market, and after the parchment shell, in which they are involved, is removed, they require but little preparation to be made into good chocolate.

HENRY.

You are not to be let off so easily, Charles, you must give us an account of the process.

CHARLES.

The Spaniards were the first that introduced the use of chocolate into Europe. The method of preparing it, first practised by them, was very simple, and the same with that in use among the Indians: they only used cacao, maize, and raw sugar, as expressed from the canes, with a little achiotl, or roco, to give it a colour: of these four drugs, ground between two stones, and mixed together in a certain proportion, they made a kind of bread, which served them equally for solid food, and for drink; eating it when hungry, and steeping it in hot water when thirsty. The Spaniards have since added many ingredients in the composition of their chocolate, which are thought to add but little to its quality. In England, the chocolate is simply ground with but little other addition than sugar and vanilla, which is the fruit of a plant cultivated in South-America. These ingredients together are made up into such cakes, as we see in the grocer's shops; when purchased for domestic use, it requires to be boiled in water, milk, or water-gruel; when sufficiently boiled, it is milled or agitated with a wooden machine for the purpose, and boiled again, in order to froth it, then mixed with sugar and cream; it forms a favourite breakfast at the table of the opulent, and serves to gratify their taste for variety.

Mr. HARCOURT.

Your account has hitherto been very entertaining; but I hope you can furnish us with the manner in which this beautiful and useful tree is cultivated, as I have been told that there are few vegetables that require more care to rear and bring to maturity.

CHARLES.

The first business of the planter is to chuse a suitable spot for the purpose. A deep black mould is the soil best adapted to the growth of the chocolate-tree; it should be a level piece of land, sheltered round with a thick wood, so as to be well screened from the wind, especially the north; after having cleared it from all manner of stumps and weeds, the planter digs a number of holes, at eighteen or twenty feet distance. Having previously selected the largest and fairest pods of the cacao, when full ripe, he takes out the grains, and puts them into a vessel of water; such of them as swim he rejects, the others, being washed clean from the pulp, and skinned, are suffered to remain in the water till they begin to sprout, when they are fit for planting. His next work is to take the leaves of the banana, or some other large leaf, one of which he places in the circumference of each hole, so as to line it within side; leaving the sides of the leaf some inches above the ground, after which he rubs the mould in very lightly, till the hole is filled; three nuts are then chosen for each hole, and planted triangularly, by making a small opening for each with his finger, about two inches deep, into which he puts the nuts with that end downwards from which the sprout issues, and having lightly covered them with mould, he folds the edges of the leaf over them, and places a small stone on the top, to prevent its opening. In the space of about eight or ten days, the young shoots begin to make their appearance above the earth, and call once more for the attendance of the planter, who unfolds the banana leaves, that the growth of the tender plant may not be impeded; in order to shelter them from the sun, other leaves or branches are placed round the hole, and they are changed as often as they decay, during five or six months. Such tender care does the cacao require, and so requisite is shade to its growth and prosperity, that, besides the precautions I have mentioned, they are obliged to plant some other tree to the south-west of the plant, which may grow up with it, and serve it for shelter against the scorching rays of the sun; the erythina, or bean-tree, is generally chosen for this purpose. In the fifth year it begins to repay the cultivator for his trouble, and by the time it has stood eight years, attains its full perfection. It generally produces two crops of fruit in the year, and will sometimes continue bearing for twenty years. The same delicacy of stamina, which characterizes its infancy, is apparent in all the stages of its growth; for it is obnoxious to blights, and shrinks from the first appearance of drought, and the greatest part of a whole crop of cacao-trees have been known to perish in a single night without any visible cause.

AUGUSTA.

I am surprised that any person has the patience and perseverance to cultivate a shrub that requires so much pains, and after all, so liable to disappoint the hopes of those who have reared it, at the expense of such a great deal of time and labour.

Mrs. HARCOURT.

I imagine that the profit it brings, when it succeeds, is the inducement to the attempt; nothing is to be effected without pains and labour; we cannot learn the simplest mechanical operation without repeated efforts; consider what numberless attempts an

153

infant makes to walk or speak, before it can either articulate a perfect sound, or proceed a few steps by itself. In the same manner, the habit of performing most of the common operations of the body, which we practise, as it were insensibly, when we have arrived at maturity, are acquired by almost imperceptible degrees: a child learns to judge of the distances of objects by experience, as of the distance and nature of sounds. The powers of smelling, tasting, feeling, hearing, and seeing, exist in a new born infant, though a considerable space of time passes, before it is capable of reaping much benefit from them; repeated and continual practice, at length enables it to see, hear, taste, feel and smell, with accuracy and precision, if it be born with perfect organs. This should teach us never to despair of attaining any degree of perfection in virtue or knowledge, of which our nature is capable. If indolence, pride, avarice, or anger, are the leading propensities of a man's disposition, let him war with determined resolution and unremitted care against that particular vice, to which he feels himself prone, and he will certainly come off victorious in the combat; resistance against a predominant inclination is at first painful, by repetition it is rendered easy, and in time the practice of the opposite virtue becomes delightful.

Mr. HARCOURT.

The possibility of overcoming vicious inclinations, and correcting what is commonly called our nature, is finely exemplified in the story of Socrates and the physiognomist. A man, who pretended to discover the characteristic marks of the disposition and affections, by the lines of the face, was introduced to Socrates, without knowing the philosopher, and desired to declare, by the rules of his art, what kind of person Socrates was. He replied, after observing his countenance attentively, that he was a drunkard, and a glutton, passionate, and a slave to vice in general. Upon which the company ridiculed his want of discernment, and denied all dependance on the truth of physiognomy; but Socrates reproved their rashness, acknowledging that in his youth he felt himself powerfully inclined to the very vices the man had named, but that perseverance and resolution had enabled him to overcome them, and all present knew that he had attained such command over himself, as to be celebrated as a model of virtue and morality. My dear Henry must lay aside his intention of entertaining us with the history of coffee, till to-morrow evening. It is too late to begin a fresh subject. Adieu; adieu.

CONVERSATION 18

Mrs. HARCOURT.

I HAVE not forgotten that little Henry is to open the conversation to night, with an account of the peculiarities of the coffee-tree. Pray, try to repeat the botanical definition properly; speak clearly and distinctly, and arrange your ideas in order; if your memory should fail, your father or Sophia will assist you with pleasure, therefore be encouraged to proceed; we are all attention.

HENRY.

After such kind encouragement from my dear mother, I have no excuse for declining the performance of my promise, though I feel myself scarcely equal to the task. The coffee-tree is a genus of the pentandria monogynia class; the flower has one petal, which is funnel shaped; it has five stamina, which are fastened to the tube, the roundish germin afterwards becomes an oval berry, containing two seeds, in shape like a half globe, flat on one side, and convex on the other. This tree originally came from Arabia Felix; but is now cultivated with success in the British West-Indies. It is a low tree, even in its native soil, seldom exceeding sixteen or eighteen feet high. In the West-India islands the negroes are employed to gather the berries; as soon as they change their colour to a dark red, they are fit for gathering. Each negro is provided with a canvass bag, with a hoop in the mouth of it, to keep it open; it is hung about the neck of the picker, who occasionally empties it into a basket; and if he be industrious, he may pick three bushels in the day. One hundred bushels in the pulp, fresh from the tree, will produce about one thousand pounds weight of merchantable coffee.

Mr. HARCOURT.

You have given us a very clear account of this tree, and the manner of gathering the berries; you must next inform us of the method used in the drying of them.

HENRY.

There are two methods in use of curing or drying the bean. The one is to spread the fresh coffee in the sun, in layers about five inches deep on a sloping terrace, or platform of boards, with the pulp on the berry, which in a few days ferments, and discharges itself in a strong acidulous moisture; and in this state the coffee is left, till it is perfectly dry, which, if the weather is favourable, it will be in about three weeks. The husks are afterwards separated from the seeds by a grinding mill, or frequently by pounding them with pestles in troughs, or large wooden mortars. The other mode is to pulp it immediately as it comes from the tree, which is done by a pulping-mill; the pulp and the bean (in its parchment skin or membrane which incloses it) fall promiscuously together; the whole is then washed in wire sieves, in order to separate the pulp from the seeds; the latter are then spread open in the sun to dry. After this follows the operation of grinding off the parchment skin, which covers the bean, and is left after the pulp is removed. When it appears sufficiently bruised, it is taken out of the trough, and put to the fan, which clears the coffee from the chaff, and the seeds remaining unground, are separated by sieves, and returned to the mill, which finishes the process.

Mrs. HARCOURT.

The coffee-berries are generally roasted before we use them. They are put into a tin cylindrical box, full of holes; through the middle of which runs a spit: beneath this machine is placed a semi-circular hearth, in which is lighted a large charcoal fire; by help of a jack the spit turns swiftly, and in that manner roasts the berries equally. When the oil rises, and is become of a dark brown colour, it is emptied into two receivers, the bottoms of which are iron plates; then the coffee is shaken, and left till almost cold; and if it looks bright and oily, it is a sign it is well done. Sophia, you are doubtless acquainted with the manner of boiling it for use.

SOPHIA.

Take a sufficient quantity of the berries for the present purpose, and grind them to a fine powder in an iron coffee-mill. Infuse this powder in a suitable proportion of boiling water, let this infusion just boil again, and stand till it is clear, and pour it off for use; the addition of cream and sugar heightens and improves the flavour.

CECILIA.

The Turks are remarkably fond of coffee; they flavour it with cloves, or essence of ambergris; and so essential do they deem it to their comfort, that it is one of the necessaries with which a Turk is obliged to furnish his wife.

Mr. HARCOURT.

Avarice has invented many substitutes for coffee; peas, beans, rye, and barley, when roasted, yield an oily matter, resembling it in a degree, but much inferior in strength and flavour.

AUGUSTA.

Many other things are sent to this country from the West-Indies, besides sugar, coffee, and chocolate.

CHARLES.

Ginger is produced there in abundance: there are three species; the first, which is the common ginger, is cultivated for sale in most of the islands in America; but is a native of the East-Indies, and also of some parts of the West-Indies, where it is found growing naturally without culture. The dried roots of this sort furnish a considerable export from the British colonies in America. The only distinction between the black and the white ginger consists in the different modes of curing the roots. The black is rendered fit for preservation by means of boiling water, and the white by exposing it to the sun; as it is necessary to select the fairest and soundest roots for this purpose, white ginger is commonly one third dearer than black in the market.

Mr. HARCOURT.

This root is planted much in the same manner as potatoes in Great Britain; but is only fit for digging once a year, unless for the purpose of preserving it in syrup. In that case it must be taken up at the end of three or four months, while its fibres are tender and full of sap.

HENRY.

Preserved ginger is a nice sweetmeat; I remember we had some of it at the entertainment given on account of Sophia's birth-day.

Mrs. HARCOURT.

Most of the preserves, that come from the West-Indies, are excellent, owing to the fineness of the sugar, of which they make the syrup, which, whilst it prevents the fruit from decaying, does not destroy its flavour, or colour.

CHARLES.

What are the principal commodities returned from England to the West-Indies, in exchange for the things we receive from thence?

Mr. HARCOURT.

The manufacturers of Birmingham and Manchester; the clothiers of Yorkshire, Gloucestershire, and Wilts; the potters of Staffordshire; the proprietors of all the lead, copper, and iron works, have a greater vent in the British West-Indies, for their respective commodities than they themselves perhaps conceive to be possible. The export of the coarser woollens to the torrid zone, for the use of the negroes, is prodigious; even sugar itself, the great staple of the West-Indies, is frequently returned them in a refined state, and thus furnishes an article of commerce in a double way.

Mrs. HARCOURT.

Commerce and traffic, either between nations or individuals, may be divided into two great articles, under one of which all the rest may be classed, viz. the raw material, or natural substances, before they are changed or transformed by the inventions of art, such as corn, wool, iron, etc. and the various productions of nature, wrought and altered into innumerable compositions, by the industry and ingenuity of man. The globe, which we inhabit, may be compared to a vast storehouse, where an infinite variety of raw materials are laid up, ready for the exercise of invention and diligence. Few things in their natural state are adapted to our use, though scarcely the meanest is void of utility, when compounded with other substances, or transformed by the action of fire, or changed by chemical processes, or wrought by manual labour; a convincing proof, that a life of sloth and inactivity is not suited to our nature, and that no rank, however exalted, is exempt from labour. The vegetable, mineral, and animal kingdoms equally contribute to furnish matter for us to work upon. You may remember that the clear, transparent, beautiful ware, we call glass, is formed only of sand and ashes; and you will presently be informed that the elegant manufacture of porcelain, or China-ware, is composed of stones. Sophia, pleased with the account of tea, coffee, and chocolate, thought the tea-equipage would be completed, by the description of the process used in making China, and in consequence, has desired me to furnish her with information on the subject, that she might be enabled to amuse you with the result.

AUGUSTA.

Stones! how is it possible to produce any thing so smooth, glossy, and delicate as China from them? and I am still more at a loss to conjecture how they can be formed into such variety of shapes and figures, or by what means they can be united into such large flat surfaces, as dishes, bowls, etc.

SOPHIA.

By first grinding them to a very fine powder, and afterwards making them into a smooth paste.

HENRY.

Paste is soft and yielding, and will not retain its shape when handled.

SOPHIA.

It must be hardened by fire, before it is in a condition for use.

CHARLES.

I have read that the Chinese, the inventors of this curious art, are extremely secret, and so jealous of the eye of strangers, that they will not allow the Europeans to go beyond the suburbs of those cities, where factories are established, lest they should discover the mysteries of their different manufactures.

Mr. HARCOURT.

That is a just representation of them. They are equally unwilling to communicate knowledge or receive instruction, and if we except the traffic carried on with the different nations of Europe at Canton, they have scarcely any intercourse with the rest of the world. Missionaries from the society of Jesuits have indeed been admitted even into Pekin, their capital city, on account of their skill in astronomical knowledge, which recommended them to the notice of the Chinese emperors and grandees, though the object of their journey was the propagation of Christianity. Most of them being men of intelligence and learning, have bestowed attention on whatever they saw, that was curious or useful, and some of them have been enabled to transmit their observations to Europe; from this source, the most authentic information on the manufacture of porcelain has been obtained, and was sent to the Grand Duke of

159

Tuscany. But Sophia, I do not intend to intrude upon your province, we expect our information from you.

SOPHIA.

It will give me great pleasure, if I am capable of affording any entertainment. The art of making porcelain is one of those in which the oriental nations have excelled the Europeans; it is chiefly manufactured in China, from whence it takes its name, but it is also brought into Europe, from other parts of the East, particularly Japan, Siam, Surat, and Persia. Neither the inventor, nor the period of its invention, is known, the Chinese annals, being silent on the subject.

Mr. HARCOURT.

Although we must acknowledge that the Orientals are superior to us in this art, yet Europe has established manufactures for several years, that have produced wares but little inferior to those of our eastern masters. The first European porcelains are said to have been made in Saxony. France followed her example, then England, afterwards Germany and Italy. Each of these manufactures differed from those of Japan and China, and respectively possess a distinct character of its own.

Mrs. HARCOURT.

Connoisseurs in porcelain have valued some of the produce of the manufacture of Meissen, a few miles from Dresden, the capital of Saxony, at even a higher rate than those of China: on account of the superior excellence of the painting and enamelling. The Saxons attribute the invention to an alchymist, named Betticher, who was confined in the castle of Koningstein, by the King of Poland, on a suspicion that he was master of the secret of the philosopher's stone, which was supposed, by credulous persons, to possess the power of converting metals into gold. Unable, with all his efforts, to obtain the subject of his researches, he employed his leisure in more useful experiments, and discovered the means of making a ware, which by its excellence and value, continues to enrich his country. His death happened in the year 1719. Among the French porcelains, that of the late king's manufactory at Sevres is the most esteemed. The Chelsea China is but little inferior to those of Saxony and France, but being expensive, and adapted chiefly to ornamental purposes, is of no very general advantage. Of the other manu-

160

factories established in this country, that of Worcester is best suited to common use, as it wears well, and comes cheap. Sophia has acquainted herself with the materials, and manner of manufacturing this commodity in the porcelain works in China, which will be sufficient to give us a general idea of the subject, without entering into the particulars of the manufactures of Europe, they being all formed upon one principle, however they may vary in minute differences.

SOPHIA.

M. Reaumur bestowed great pains in analysing the component parts of the eastern China, and found that it consisted of two substances, one of which is easily vitrified, or converted into glass, the other possessing a contrary quality; the combination of those opposite materials produces porcelain, which is a half vitrified substance or manufacture, in a middle state, between the common baked earthen-ware of our coarse manufactures, and true glass. This composition makes a very curious article in commerce, and not less so in natural history. In order to proceed with method, I shall consider four things; the materials that compose it; the art of giving the proper figure and shape to the different works; the colours with which it is painted, gilded, and enamelled; and lastly, the baking, or exposing it to the proper degree of fire. There are two kinds of earths, and as many different oils, or varnishes, used in the composition of porcelain. The first earth, called kaolin, is intermixed with glittering corpuscles; the second, named petunse, is plain white, but exceedingly fine. They are both found in quarries twenty or thirty leagues from Kingteching, the name of the town where the most considerable China-works are carried on, and to this place, these earths, or rather stone, are brought in a number of little barks, incessantly passing up and down the river Iaotcheou for that purpose. The petunses are cut from the quarries in form of bricks, being naturally pieces of a very hard rock; those are mostly valued, of which the colour inclines to a greenish hue. The first preparation of these bricks is to break and pound them, till they are rendered impalpable, or as fine as can be conceived. This powder is thrown into an urn, full of water, and stirred briskly about with an iron instrument. After letting it stand still a while, the lighter parts of the powder form a skim on the surface of the water, several inches thick, which the workmen carefully skim off into another vessel filled with water, leaving the heavier sediment at the bottom to be reground. The second vessel is left to settle, and when it has stood long enough, they pour off the clear water, and reserve the matter, which subsides, for use: when it is nearly dry, it is cut into square pieces, and afterwards mixed with kaolin in proper proportion. The kaolin is much softer than the petunse, when dug out of the quarry; yet this is the ingredient, which, by its mixture with the other, gives strength and firmness to the work. The mountains, whence the kaolin is dug, are covered on the outside surface with a reddish earth. The mines are deep, and the matter is found in glebes or clods. They prepare both these stones in a similar manner.

CHARLES.

Pottery in general is made of clays or argillaceous earths, because they are capable of being kneaded, and easily receive any form, and acquire solidity and hardness, by exposure to the fire; but I observe that porcelain is formed of the hardest rocks, reduced to an artificial clay or paste, by grinding them fine, and softening them with liquids.

SOPHIA.

The oils, that are added, soften them, I suppose, in a still greater degree, and render their texture smooth and uniform. The first oil or varnish is a whitish liquid substance, drawn from the hard stone of which the petunses are formed; they chuse the whitest squares, and those that have the most streaks of green in them for making the oil; they prepare the petunses for this purpose in the same manner as for making squares; when reduced to this state, it is mixed with a mineral stone, called shekau or kehao, resembling alum, which they first heat red hot, and then reduce into an impalpable powder; this gives the oil a consistence, but it should not be made too thick, as it is still to be kept in a liquid state. The fourth ingredient is the oil of lime, which requires a more tedious and difficult process. After dissolving large pieces of quick lime, and reducing them to a powder, by sprinkling water on them, they put a layer of fern on this powder, and on the fern, another of the slacked lime, and so on alternately, till they have heaped a moderate pile, to which they set fire; when the whole is consumed, they compose another pile of layers of the ashes, and new layers of dry fern, which they burn as before; this operation is repeated five or six times, the oil being reckoned better, the oftener the ashes are burned. A quantity of these ashes of fern and lime is thrown into an urn filled with water, and to one hundred pounds of ashes is added one pound of shekau, which dissolves in it; the rest of the process is the same as in preparing the earth of the petunses; the sediment found at the bottom of the second urn, kept in a liquid state, is called the oil of lime, from which the porcelain derives its principal lustre.

CECILIA.

I am not surprised at the superiority of porcelain to common earthen ware, now I am acquainted with the various processes used to render the materials suitable to the elegant purpose for which they are designed.

Mrs. HARCOURT.

As you have described the materials of this manufacture, and the manner of preparing them for their several uses, we must be contented to reserve the account of the various methods of forming them into vessels, figures, etc. till a future opportunity, as a particular engagement obliges me to leave you rather earlier than usual this evening.

CONVERSATION 19

AUGUSTA.

MY father has promised to take me to-morrow, to see a gentleman's museum, which is filled with rarities and valuable curiosities; among other things, he tells me that there are several philosophical instruments, and that I am to see a variety of experiments. I should anticipate a great deal of pleasure in this visit, were I not entirely ignorant of the subjects with which I am to be entertained; so many things arise in my mind, which I wish to enquire about, lest I should expose my ignorance before strangers, that I find it difficult to select the questions most necessary to ask.

Mrs. HARCOURT.

A consciousness of our defects is the first step towards improvement; a young lady of your age is not expected to be deeply skilled in philosophy; much less to display her knowledge, should she possess a small share; but a general acquaintance with the uses of the most common philosophical instruments is not only ornamental, but also a very useful accomplishment, and should form part of every liberal education.

AUGUSTA.

My father mentioned several particulars, that are to be shewn me; telescopes, microscopes, and an orrery especially; but I am quite unacquainted with the purposes to which any of them are applied.

Mr. HARCOURT.

In order to prepare your mind for your intended visit, we will defer our conclusion of the porcelain manufacture till our next meeting, and endeavour to explain the uses to which some of the most common philosophical instruments are applied. To enter into a description of their construction, or an explanation of their parts, would be uninteresting and tedious, unless we had the machines before us. We will begin with the telescope, as presenting the most conspicuous, important, and noble objects in nature. It is an optical instrument, consisting of several glasses or lenses, fitted into a tube, through which remote objects are viewed as if near. Before the invention of the telescope, the wonders of the heavens were concealed from us beyond the powers of the naked eye; and astronomy, that exalted science, which illustrates the Omnipotence of the Divine Creator of the universe more eminently than any other branch of human knowledge, has been improved, and brought, by this simple instrument, to a degree of perfection unthought of, in former ages. The discovery was owing to chance rather than reflection, as it is certain, that the theory, upon which it depends, was not known when the first telescopes were made. Several claimed the honour of the invention; but Galileo, in the beginning of the seventeenth century, having been told of a certain optic glass made in Holland, which brought distant objects nearer to the eye, considered by what means this effect could be produced, and grinding two pieces of glass into form as well as he could, fitted them to the ends of an organ pipe, and with this indifferent apparatus shewed at once the novelty and wonder of the invention to the Venetian noblesse, on the top of the tower of St. Mark. From this time Galileo devoted himself wholly to the improving and perfecting of the telescope, and by his perseverance deserved the honour, usually attributed to him, of being the inventor of the instrument, and of its receiving the denomination of Galileo's tube, from his name. The Doge of Venice rewarded his assiduity with the ducal letters, and doubled his salary.

Mrs. HARCOURT.

The extraordinary talents of this great man improved the first invention of the telescope to a vast degree of perfection; but it has been reserved for the period, in which we live, to advance the magnifying powers to a height at once truly astonishing. Our contemporary, Dr. Herschel has made surprising progress in celestial geography, if I may be allowed the expression, by means of his Newtonian seven feet reflector, the most powerful instrument of the kind ever seen. It has enabled him to discover many stars before unknown, and curious particulars relative to those, with which we were previously acquainted.

CHARLES.

When the immense and inconceivable distances of the fixed stars are considered, it is wonderful to reflect that the inventive powers, of such a diminutive animal as man, have ever attained to such degrees of information on a subject apparently so far beyond his reach.

HENRY.

I do not think that the stars are so very far distant. On a clear night I have observed them but a little way above my head. I have tried several times to count them, but they are so numerous that I have always found it impossible.

CHARLES.

You are much deceived, my dear brother, in both respects. The stars, that are visible to the naked eye, are not so numerous as we are apt to suppose, from viewing them in a confused irregular manner; a thousand is supposed to be the greatest number ever seen in our hemisphere at one time, by the keenest eye, and most attentive observer. Their extreme distance conceals them from our sight, except they are unveiled by the assistance of telescopes, for they are really numerous beyond our limited imagination to conceive; and in order to give you a faint idea of their vast distance, I will relate a few observations, that I have heard upon the subject. Nothing, that we know, is so swift in its passage as light; a ray of light passes from the sun to the earth in eight minutes and thirteen seconds, a distance of ninety-five millions, one hundred and twenty-three thousand miles; and yet, though possessing this amazing velocity, it would be one year and a quarter traversing the space between us and the nearest fixed star. A cannon ball, discharged from a twenty-four pounder with two-thirds of its weight of powder, moves at about the rate of nineteen miles in a minute, but would be seven hundred and sixty thousand years passing from the nearest fixed star to our earth. Sound, which travels at the rate of nearly thirteen miles in a minute, would be one million, one hundred and twenty thousand years in passing through the same space.

CECILIA.

How far does the structure of the universe, viewed in this light, exceed the bounds of the strongest imagination! well might David express his sense of those wonders, by exclaiming, that the heavens declare the glory of God, and the firmament sheweth his handy work.

SOPHIA.

Addison remarks, that the universe is the work of infinite power, prompted by infinite goodness, having an infinite space to exert itself in, so that our imagination can set no limits to it.

Mrs. HARCOURT.

The microscope is an instrument calculated to shew the other extreme of nature's works, by magnifying very minute objects, so as to render that clear to the sight which, from its minuteness, was before imperceptible. Dr. Hooke, who has written on the microscope, divides the objects proper to be viewed by it into three classes, which he calls exceeding small bodies, exceeding small pores, and exceeding small motions. Small bodies must either be the parts of larger bodies, or things, the whole of which is too minute for our observation, unassisted by art; such as small seeds, insects, salts, sands, &c. Very small pores are the interstices between the solid parts of bodies, as in stones, timbers, minerals, shells, &c. or the mouths of minute vessels in vegetables, or the pores in the skin, bones, and other parts of animals. Extreme small motions are the movements of the several parts or members of minute animals, or the motion of the fluids, contained in either animal or vegetable bodies. Under one or other of these three heads, almost every thing around us affords matter of observation, and may conduce to our amusement and instruction.

AUGUSTA.

From what I have heard this evening, I expect to be highly entertained to-morrow, and hope, on some future day, you will favour me with more information on these subjects.

Mr. HARCOURT.

It always affords me peculiar pleasure to communicate any thing to you, my dear children, that may enlarge and exalt your ideas of the great first Cause, from whom every thing proceeds, and by whom every thing is arranged and governed in the most perfect order; whether we reflect on the heavenly bodies, those stupendous instances of his omnipotence; or consider the insect imperceptible by its minuteness, yet perfect in all its parts, both internal and external, we are led equally to admire and adore the same power, wisdom and goodness, that are manifested in each extreme of his works.

167

Mrs. HARCOURT.

The order of the universe is an inexhaustible theme of wonder and admiration to all, who consider it attentively; the wisest and most virtuous men of all ages have uniformly agreed in admiring the connection of its parts, and the correspondence of means to the end designed. Of what use would the eye have been, with all its curious mechanism, if there had been no light to render objects visible? The more extensive our knowledge of nature, the more capable we are of tracing the wisdom and intelligence, that are visible in every part of the creation.

CHARLES.

Notwithstanding the harmony of the works of Providence is so obvious to the most superficial observer, I have heard that there have been men so perversely stupid, as to suppose, that this beautiful world, with all its various inhabitants, as well as the other parts of the universe, were produced by mere chance, or the accidental assemblage of atoms, and have refused to acknowledge the existence of one Supreme Intelligent Being.

Mrs. HARCOURT.

If any man indeed ever doubted of that awful truth, he must have first bewildered his mind in useless and unprofitable speculations on metaphysical and abstruse subjects, beyond our limited capacities to explore, and ill suited to make us either wiser or better.

SOPHIA.

Let such an one observe the texture of the simplest blade of grass, the gauze wing of a common fly, without extending his researches to the economy of either the animal or vegetable world, and try if it can be imitated by the most exquisite specimens of art, he will find that it baffles every attempt, even in its external structure; but when he examines the internal organization and uses of the parts, he must acknowledge it to be the work of a Divine Artist.

Mr. HARCOURT.

The various degrees of instinct in animals, and the intellectual powers in man, will be still more difficult to account for, as originating from any inferior cause, than that of an Infinitely Wise Almighty Being.

Mrs. HARCOURT.

Natural religion, or the belief of the existence of a God, the Creator and Preserver of the Universe, for the manifestation of his power, wisdom and goodness, is not confined to the globe which we inhabit, but extends to the remotest point of created space, is so congenial to our rational nature, that it is surprising that any one ever dared to acknowledge a doubt of it.

Mr. HARCOURT.

The united testimony of all ages and nations concurs to render such men suspected of professing a belief which in the privacy of their own minds they deny, or of wilfully refusing to open their understandings to the convictions of truth. The most savage and ignorant tribes in every part of the globe, not only acknowledge the existence of a Supreme Cause, though they worship him under different names, and frequently mistake very absurd objects for his representatives; but also an universal belief of his divine influence upon the human mind; from this conviction arises the idea of prayer, a custom confined to no particular country, but the universal refuge of the human species in moments of distress and anguish; an assurance, that he graciously condescends to hear the petitions of his creatures, and benevolently relieves their affliction, must give encouragement to these applications.

Mrs. HARCOURT.

If we deprive mankind of this consoling hope, our present state is a deplorable one indeed; beset with temptations, surrounded by difficulties and trials, to what power could we flee for succour? Wretchedness with despair would be thy portion, O man! bereft of the consolation of natural religion, which not only teaches us to believe in the existence of an Almighty God, but also to adore his infinite perfections, to rely upon his goodness for preservation from the evils of the present life; and prepares us for the reception of the truths of revealed religion, by which are meant those manifestations, which have been revealed to man supernaturally by various means, but in a most especial manner by the coming of Jesus Christ, who was sent on earth to introduce a more pure and holy religion than that given to the Jews, or any that had ever been contrived by human wisdom. He might properly be called the messenger of glad tidings, offering peace and immortality to all the human race without distinction, who should embrace his doctrine, and live according to his precepts.

Mr. HARCOURT.

The perverseness of men's dispositions, and the limited faculties we possess, whilst in our present state, will ever raise cavillers against the most clear conviction; but let us shut our ears against their conversation, and our eyes against their writings; contenting ourselves with the study of the New Testament, and relying upon the assurances the Gospel offers; convinced that this line of conduct cannot injure us, but is likely to lead us to peace and happiness.

Mrs. HARCOURT.

The period of man's life is too short to be wasted in speculative researches, which have no influence in correcting the disposition, or amending the heart. The path of duty is plain and obvious to every one who sincerely endeavours to find it, and is equally adapted to the capacity of the unlettered hind, as to that of the learned philosopher. Each one has a part to perform, according to the circumstances in which he is placed; superior intelligence calls for superior excellence. A disposition to acknowledge the goodness of the Supreme Being towards all the parts of his creation, and thanksgiving for the peculiar blessings bestowed on each individual are incumbent duties on every rational creature. Let us unite in offering this incense with unfeigned gratitude, and conclude this conversation in the words of the poet;

> Almighty power, amazing are thy ways,
> Above our knowledge, and above our praise;
> How all thy works thy excellence display!
> How fair, how wonderful are they!
> Thy hand yon wide extended heaven uprais'd,
> Yon wide extended heaven with stars emblaz'd,
> When each bright orb, since Time his course begun,
> Has roll'd a mighty world, or shin'd a sun.
> Stupendous thought! how sinks all human race,
> A point, an atom, in the field of space.
> Yet e'en to us, O Lord, thy care extends,
> Thy bounty feeds us, and thy power defends.
> Yet ev'n to us, as delegate of thee,
> Thou giv'st dominion over land and sea.
> Whate'er or walks on earth, or flits in air,

Whate'er of life the watery regions bear,
All these are ours, and for th'extensive claim,
We owe due homage to thy sacred name.
Almighty Power, how wond'rous are thy ways!
How far above our knowledge and our praise!